MARCO POLO

BRUSSELS

There are five symbols to help you find your way around this guide:

★
Marco Polo's top recommendations – the best in each category

sites with a scenic view

places where the local people meet

places where young people get together

(100/A1)
pages and coordinates for the Street Atlas of Brussels
(U/A1) *coordinates for the Brussels area map on the inside front cover*
(O) *area not covered by maps*

This guide was written by Siggi Weidemann.
He is a foreign correspondent and author of books about Belgium.

Cover photograph: Grand' Place, Guildhalls (Schuster/Pöche)
Photos: Author (73); Knigge (9, 22, 24, 27, 34, 40, 42, 45, 46, 49, 60, 63, 66, 80, 85, 87, 95); laif: Hahn (53, 55); Mauritius: Ley (99), Torino (56), Troisfontaines (18), Vidler (7); Schapowalow: Heaton (14), Messerschmidt (19), Valdin (23, 76, 79); D. Scherf (4); Silvestris: Stadler (11, 13, 33, 96)

1st edition 2000

Translator: Rosemary Quinton
English edition 2000: Margaret Court
Editorial director: Ferdinand Ranft
Chief editor: Marion Zorn
Cartography for the Street Atlas: © Falk-Verlag, Stuttgart
Design and layout: Thienhaus/Wippermann
Printed in Germany

CONTENTS

Discover Brussels!

The European Union's bilingual capital has a style all of its own, shaped by a thousand years of history, art and culture

Visitors to the city of Brussels, which likes to be known as "the heart of Europe", cannot fail to be impressed by its southern charm and complete lack of affectation. The capital of Belgium is straightforward and unpretentious, its inhabitants reserved but friendly, and pragmatic. Brussels, which stands for a whole way of life in which art , culture and cooking co-exist in happy symbiosis, is nowadays a centre of attraction for architects and gourmets, comic-strip enthusiasts, music lovers, young people, and anyone who likes flea markets.

But there is more to Brussels than this: it is a many-sided enigma, the culmination of a thousand years of history, a city of contrasts whose cosmopolitan inhabitants, full of *joie de vivre*, rub shoulders with more conservative citizens, a city characterized by Gothic façades and glass palaces. A capital city, with a wealth of art treasures collected by emperors, kings, dukes and self-assured citizens. It has one of Europe's most famous squares, the Grand' Place, where pavement cafés invite you to linger over a coffee and contemplate your surroundings in peace: a gem set in stone, or, as the French poet Jean Cocteau described it "the most beautiful scenery in the world". Where better to get the feel of this city of contradictions? According to a survey carried out by the French magazine "L'Express", Brussels has the highest standard of living of any European capital except Paris.

Until the late 1980s the bilingual capital of the highly individual kingdom of Belgium was overshadowed by other European capitals. Then increasing numbers of signs bearing the word "Renovation" started to appear. A large number of historical buildings – of which Brussels has many – are still hidden behind scaffolding or awnings. A wave of investment is underway, which should carry Brussels well into the future. It now occupies third place amongst international conference centres, and some six million visitors travel there annually to form their own impressions of this pulsating European metropolis. However,

The view of the old city from the Mont des Arts. Brussels has been a capital city since time immemorial

Brussels is by no means a melting pot. The various cultural and linguistic groups mostly live in their own quarters where they lead their own way of life: and each community still follows its own customs and traditions.

Most German, English, French or Spanish people live in the fashionable, green suburbs such as Tervuren, Overijse or Wezembeek, Moroccans and Turks in Schaerbeek or St-Josse, and Afrikaners at Porte Namur.

Brussels lies in the geographical centre of the country and is one of the many-layered European towns built on the hills of Brabant. It is believed to have been founded in about AD 580 on an island in the Senne, and in the 12th century was rebuilt on higher ground. In the late Middle Ages it was at the political centre of Europe, the emperor had his residence in the Palace, and the guilds demonstrated their power with their gold-painted guildhalls. The Palais de Justice, built on the medieval gallows hill, is a monument to chivalric authority. It was intended to epitomise the skills of European masterbuilders. The oppressive gloominess of this fearsome edifice, the largest to be built in Brussels in the nineteenth century, is enough to make even the most enlightened visitor shudder. The wealth of the city also manifests itself in other symbols of greatness and power: there is the Grand' Place, architecturally the most spectacular market place in the world; there is an outstanding collection of old masters in the Musée de l'Art Ancien and a wonderful park, the Forêt des Soignes; there is Waterloo, one of the most famous battlefields in world history, and the old quarter, Ilôt Sacré, popularly known as the "belly of Brussels" thanks to its high concentration of restaurants. Brussels, the heart and centre of Europe, occupies an area of about 16,179 hectares, with green spaces accounting for some 15 per cent.

Brussels has grown out of 19 communes, and each area of the city preserves its own independence. The largest of the communes, each of which has its own administration, is the Commune de Bruxelles in the city centre. Some 140,000 people live in the centre, whilst Greater Brussels has a population of about 952,200, more than a quarter of whom are foreigners. Greater Brussels is one of the three federal regions of the Belgian State, with a prime minister at its head. The city is officially bilingual, which is evident from the street names, notices in public transport and on the streets. French Walloons make up some four-fifths of the inhabitants, and Dutch-speaking Flemings the rest. Brussels is a French-speaking island in the middle of the Flemish province of Brabant, and the city's culture, politics and economy show strong Flemish influence. Since 1989 Brussels has been the seat of the Flemish government. A city of linguistic and political compromises, and hence a place full of irritations.

Brussel, Bruxelles, Bruocsella. This multi-lingual city, in which the dialects of Dutch and French speakers are mixed up together, is a place of many peoples and cultures, colourful and hectic, poor and well-to-do. A place where absurdities of all kinds lie

The Maison du Roi is a unique example of Brabant gothic architecture

in wait for the unsuspecting visitor. No one has expressed this so well as René Magritte (1898-1967). His home city provided the raw material of surrealism, since everything that actually was, could just as well be different. His manner of painting captured the essential mood of Brussels: a longing for space. Magritte denied reality and turned facts on their heads (or back on their feet), he neutralized gravity, and turned living things to stone. Better than anyone, this celebrated painter personifies Brussels, this city where there is certainly no lack of dream worlds.

Where the fine things of life are concerned, Brussels has more than its fair share. A visit will naturally begin with the famous attractions: the Grand' Place, Manneken Pis, Atomium, Parc du Cinquantenaire, the Marolles district or the comic-strip museum. Equally essential is a visit to one of the better restaurants of which the capital is generously supplied. Brussels is not only a centre for the arts, but also a metropolis of culinary discoveries, of which mussels with chips is only one famous example.

It is impossible to really understand the city, known as

Brussels – capital of the European Union

Whilst British Members of Parliament meet by the Thames at Westminster to debate and make decisions, several hundred miles away, across the English Channel, the Members of the European Parliament are working on the future of Europe. For a long time now, some 40 per cent of all decisions that also concern the individual nations, have been taken centrally in Europe. Regional politicians no longer turn to their own governments when they want money, but directly to Brussels, from where generous grant aid is handed out. Brussels is a magnet as much to young talent in general as to aspiring politicians. This city may once have been a mere supply post, but it is now a centre with plenty of highly paid jobs. Even so it would be true to say that the general public is largely left out in the cold by the whole European project.

Half of all Europeans have never even heard or read anything about the work of the European Parliament. This is scarcely surprising, since there is no such thing as a European Government and certainly no genuine feeling of European identity. People regard themselves as Portuguese, Danish or German, for instance. There is no European nation as such, and hence no European Parliament that really deserves the name. And yet, every five years the citizens of the European Union are called upon to elect 626 EU delegates. The United Kingdom sends 87 representatives, compared with the 99 sent by Germany, which has the largest population of any EU country. The Members of the European Parliament meet either in Luxembourg, Strasbourg or Brussels. They have to agree the EU budget and to comment on the legislative proposals put forward by the Commission, which they have the power to dismiss with a two-thirds majority.

The European Union (EU) brings together the member states of the European Economic Community, which was initially formed in 1954, when its founder members decided that its headquarters should be in Brussels. The European Community became the European Union in 1993, when the Treaty of Maastricht came into force. In 1996 the decision was taken to introduce the Euro, and in 1999 the fifth election to the European Parliament was held.

Brussels is the headquarters of the EU Commission, which consists of one representative from every EU country, or two in the case of larger countries. The commission puts forward proposals for European legislation and is responsible for implementing policy decided upon, and for ensuring free competition. The EU Council of Ministers also has its permanent base in Brussels.

More than 50,000 jobs are directly connected with the European authorities, and there are a further quarter of a million which are indirectly dependent on the EU employees, the thousands of lobbyists, government-dependent organisations, associations, trade unions, approximately 160 embassies, and large numbers of representatives from the regions. The city's economic life therefore swallows up several billion every year.

If you would like to visit the European Parliament, write to the Visitor Service at *Belliardstraat 97–113, B–1047 Brussels, Fax 0032/2/284 35 30.*

the Lady of Europe, and perhaps even to fall in love with it, without finding out about Brussels' eventful history. The original settlement of Bruocsella (place in the swamp) developed into a town in the 11th century, after Charles of Lorraine, on the orders of Emperor Otto II, erected a fortress at the crossing of the trade routes from Cologne to Paris and Bruges. The city rapidly grew into what was, in medieval terms, a metropolis, with 40,000 inhabitants inside its city walls. After the Counts of Louvain and later the Dukes of Brabant built their fortress on the hill known as the "Coudenberg" and started work on building the cathedral, Brussels became the most important commercial town in the dukedom of Brabant and the course was set for its subsequent prosperity: the textile industry flourished, the guilds became powerful and received the power of the keys over the city gates. Towards the middle of the 14th century work started on the building of a second city wall, which lasted until the 18th century when Napoleon ordered its demolition to make way for a bypass, the present-day inner ring. The city gate Port de Hal and the black tower of St. Catherine's church are all that is left of the former mighty bulwarks.

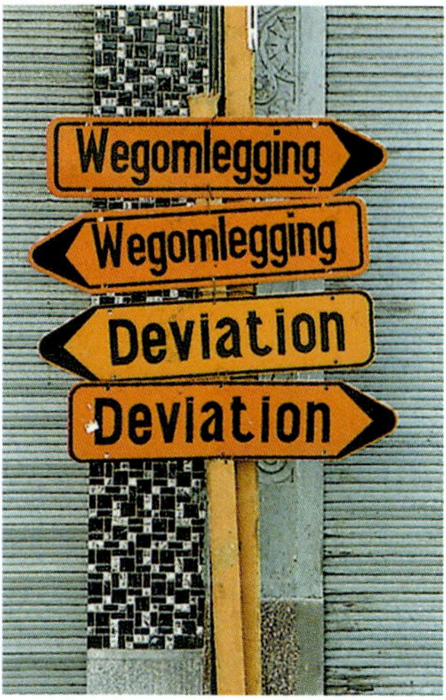

The fact that Brussels is bi-lingual is not the only cause of confusion

Guilds and merchants received political influence in 1421 when the Grand' Place, hitherto inhabited by noble families, was made accessible to craftsmen, and a prosperous middle class emerged. Thus guildhalls were built by fishmongers, merchants, and sailors on inland waterways, whilst the nobility built new palaces on the Coudenberg. As a symbol of the newly acquired rights of the merchants and craftsmen, the Hôtel de Ville (city hall) was built on the Grand' Place, the church of Notre Dame de la Chapelle was built, and the cathedral was completed. Under the Dukes of Burgundy the city then experienced a commercial and creative boost. The achievements of cities such as Ghent, Mechelen, Antwep, Bruges, Louvain and Damme put Flanders on a par with the cities of Upper Italy, as an historical area where art and science especially flourished in the 14th and 15th centuries. There was a lively trade and exchange of goods between these two countries. Flemish artists, painters, sculptors and architects drew inspiration from the south, whilst Italians came to Flanders to be inspired in their turn.

In 1490 a postal connection was established between Innsbruck and Brussels, after Brussels fell to the Habsburgs and the Burgundians withdrew. And Brussels can count itself lucky in that Emperor Charles V, who was born in Ghent, made the city his seat of government so that it became the capital of the Spanish Netherlands in 1531. At that time Brussels already had a population of 70,000.

The period during which present-day Flanders and Spain were ruled over by the Habsburgs has gone down in history as the "Golden Century". During the reign of Charles V (1500–58) as Holy Roman Emperor and as Charles I King of Spain, two important events occurred: the Reformation in Germany and the conquest of the Spanish colonial empire in Central and South America. Charles V ruled over the colonies in America, the Netherlands, Portugal, the Philippines and large parts of Italy. In Schiller's play "Don Carlos" Charles is heard to cry out: "The sun never sets on my kingdom". However conflicts with the Protestants and the Calvinists, the struggles against the Turks, four wars against his rivals and quarrels with France and England, not to mention the subsequent privateering war of the Dutch against the Spanish silver fleets were in the end to lead to a Spanish decline, and the religious war with the Dutch to Brussels' economic stagnation. The widely dispersed countries were difficult to govern, the postal and trade routes long and dangerous. The "Spanish route" to Brussels led from Barcelona to Genoa (by ship), then on to Milan, Besançon and Luxembourg. But whenever Charles V stayed in his Palace on the Coudenberg, Brussels could regard itself as the hub of the world, and Christendom was governed from Flanders.

Following Charles V's abdication in favour of his son Philip II in Brussels in 1526, and his withdrawal into the Spanish monastery at Yuste, the dark ages of the Spanish occupation began. In 1567 the Duke of Alba became governor of the Netherlands, and the 80-year-long war between Spain and the Netherlands began. Pieter Bruegel, who lived and worked in the Marolles district, condemned the "Spanish fury" in his picture "The Holy Innocents". In 1568 Counts Hoorne and Egmont were beheaded on the Grand' Place for alleged conspiracy. In the mean time the Reformation had also won support in Flanders, resulting in iconoclasm. William I, Prince of Orange and Count of Nassau, who wished to resolve the conflict peacefully, however sided with the rebels. More than 100,000 people fled to the northern Netherlands where cultural and economic life flourished – whilst Brussels degenerated into a province.

At the beginning of the 17th century the city enjoyed a brief period of prosperity during the rule of Archduke Albrecht and his wife Isabella. Once again houses and churches were built, this time in Italian classical style.

In 1695, during the nine-years war the city was heavily bombarded on the orders of Louis XIV, the Sun King, and the centre of the lower city was razed to the ground. More than 4,000 houses were destroyed. The Grand' Place as we know it today dates from the years following this, around 1700.

Prince Eugène, the Viennese hero of the war against the Turks, became governor of the Austrian Netherlands in 1716. The people of Brussels protested against this re-imposition of foreign rule, and Prince Eugène retaliated with all the power of the Empire: in 1719 he had Frans Anneessens, dean of the guilds and leader in the struggle for freedom, beheaded.

In 1725 peace was restored under the governance of Archduchess Maria Elisabeth, but it was only under Charles Alexander of Lorraine that Brussels experienced a return to prosperity. By the time of the French Revolution in 1789 a large part of the city had been built in classical style. The castle and the palaces around the Coudenberg were rebuilt and the Place des Martyrs was laid out. As a result of the French Revolution the people of Brussels drove out the Austrians, but from 1794 the city, along with the rest of Belgium and Holland, came under French rule. After the Battle of Waterloo in 1815 and the fall of Napoleon, Belgium was ruled by Orange and Brussels became the second city, after the Hague, in the new Kingdom of the Netherlands. Yet again the people of Brussels took up arms against

The Lion Monument looking over the battlefield at Waterloo

their new oppressors and on 25 August 1830, Brussels was the scene of insurrection. The Belgian Revolution broke out, the Dutch were driven out, and Brussels again became the capital of an independent kingdom. In 1831 Leopold of Saxe-Coburg became the first king of the Belgians. Development in the new capital now took place at a rapid pace. In 1834 Brussels got its own university and a year later the first railway on the continent of Europe was opened, between Brussels and Mechelen. The city's remaining fortifications were demolished, many historic buildings disappeared and the great boulevards were laid out. The city, whose population now numbered about 100,000 was building for the future.

The city's image reflects its varied history, with the most enduring changes to the capital having been made by Emperor Leopold II, who came to the throne in 1865 and invested enthusiastically in building projects. Inspired by colonial France and England Leopold II set about industrialization, based on the exploitation of his African colony, the Belgian Congo. As the Brussels government had no wish to follow the king in his colonial adventure, Leopold bought two million square kilometres of the Congo (later Zaire) from his own private purse. The Royal Palaces in Brussels and Laeken, the boulevards, modelled on those of Paris, the Parc du Cinquantenaire ("Jubilee Park"), the hothouses and the magnificent Avenue de Tervuren, leading to the Royal Museum of Central Africa, testify to these acquisitions, as the Palais de Justice does to an exaggerated sense of self-confidence.

The law courts building, designed by Joseph Peolaert and built from 1866–83, and far larger than St. Peter's in Rome, stands like a fortress overlooking the Marolles quarter, a district which has changed rapidly in recent years. The streets around the "Vossenplein" have been the haunt of ordinary people since time immemorial. However recent developments have not left this part of the city untouched; although nowhere else in Brussels are there so many plain, unpretentious pubs or dusty second-hand shops, and nowhere else is the native wit of Brussels so strongly in evidence. If protests are to be made anywhere in the capital against bad town planning or against the vagaries of officialdom, this is the place. But so far it has been of little avail to the inhabitants. Like other districts of the city, the heart of the city counts as one of the most neglected quarters. Grievances are openly aired in the media, but this self-criticism only makes the public the feel powerless. In the inner city alone, 140 protected buildings have fallen victim to the demolition hammer. The inhabitants' rage against the speculators and the city fathers as well as the fat cats of the EU for whom the Marolles is "the" place to live, is becoming clearer and shriller.

In 1914 and 1940 Belgium was a theatre of war, with Brussels under German occupation but the city escaped being badly destroyed. In 1951 King Leopold III had to abdicate and the country was then reigned over by his son Baudouin I of Saxe-Coburg. Baudoin, the fifth King of Belgium, died, childless, on 31 July 1993. Albert II, his brother has since then reigned as "Father of the Fatherland".

Women have always played an important role in the history of Brussels; not only the cultivated abbesses, of the nunneries of Brussels, but also the queens and female governors, who ruled the country from Brussels. For 21 years the fate of the city lay in the hands of Johanna of Brabant (1322–1406), and other famous figures include Maria of Burgundy (1458–82), Margaret of Austria, Maria of Hungary and the Infanta Isabella. For about 150 years, from the 16th to the 18th century, women resided in the Royal Palace in Brussels. It is thanks to them that so much refinement was introduced into the life of Brussels, where art and literature are still highly rated. Juliette Drouet, who followed her lover Victor Hugo into exile in Brussels was attracted by the city's liberality and its appreciation of the arts. Karl Marx, who married the sweetheart of his youth, Jenny von Westphalen in 1843, spent three years in Brussels. Tradition has it that Jenny Marx was infuriated by the blatant social inequalities here. She is said to have protested vehemently when the elegant "Galeries Saint-Hubert" were opened, whilst people were starving in the poorer quarters.

To discover the many faces of Brussels takes a little time. Much is hidden, and you need to look carefully to get a true impression, as the city is in the process of acquiring a new face. The policy of "Brusselization", the brutal transformation and destruction of the city, has now given way to the subtle art of "façadism". This means that classical buildings are no longer pulled down, but architecturally valuable façades are kept, and new buildings put up behind them. Thus the congress centre and the glass palace of the European Parliament tower above the protected station façade. There are reasons to hope that the remains of the Quartier Léopold, the elegant quarter dating from the turn of the 19th/20th century, may still be rescued. Perhaps those campaigning to make Brussels a more pleasant place to live in will in due course have their own monument, like the one erected to Everard t'Serclaes, in 1356 the "Defender of the City's Freedom", in the form of a relief: a panel on the Maison L'Etoile (Grand' Place) depicts three important events from the city's history. The eye is drawn particularly to the arm of the martyr t'Serclaes, gleaming like gold because it has been grasped by so many visitors – for legend has it that anyone who touches this arm will have good luck for a year. And who would not want a year of good luck? That prospect alone makes the trip to Brussels worth while.

The EU building, currently closed for building work

SUMMER HOUSE

Exploring the city

It is the contrasts that make Brussels such a lively place: art nouveau and medieval treasures, narrow alleyways and smart avenues

Slowly, hesitatingly, Brussels reveals itself to the visitor. Whether travelling by car or by train, the approach to the city leads through its less salubrious corners, which stand in sharp contrast to the heart of the city. The enormous growth of the European metropolis is evident from the numerous excavations and cranes, the hectic pace of life, the hustle and bustle. For years the city has been a paradise for speculators and developers who had to satisfy the huge demand for office space and homes for the Eurocrats, lobbyists, journalists and officials. The administration of Europe meant flying the flag of wholesale redevelopment and agricultural consolidation. This process has been dubbed "Bruxellesation" ("Brusselization"). Gleaming, glass tower blocks have sprung up overnight in quarters which grew up gradually over the course of centuries of history. The contrast between old and new is great. But for some time now the preservation of ancient buildings has again been taken seriously, and work has been carried out on renovation and restoration. Brussels shines with a new lustre, as befits the capital of United Europe.

A symbol of the atomic age and a landmark of Brussels: the 102 m high Atomium

Brussels' architectural heritage reflects its varied and eventful history: it was the capital of the Counts of Brabant and the Dukes of Burgundy. And Charles V, also known as King Carlos I of Spain, born in Ghent, on whose kingdom the "sun never set" was proclaimed ruler here by the Spanish in 1516. Brussels was also a city of the Inquisition, and at different times it belonged to the Habsburgs, to France and to Holland. There are still numerous buildings in the classical style, dating back to that period: the Grand' Place is the central point of all the architectural attractions, of which Brussels still has a great many. A peculiar feature of town planning is that Brussels has been divided into the upper and lower city. The lower city, which lies only 15–20 m above sea level, extends out around the Grand' Place, the Stock Exchange and the Marché aux Herbes ("grass market"). Thirty metres above its highest point begins the upper city, with the Place Madon and Duden

Park, which lies 50–100 m above sea level.

Nearly all the sights are to be found in the city centre and can easily be reached on foot. Places of interest on the edge of the city, such as the Parc du Cinquantenaire ("Jubilee Park") and the Atomium can be comfortably reached by Metro or taxi. Brussels taxi drivers are considered friendly.

ART NOUVEAU/ART DECO

At the end of the 19th century Europe was gripped by a movement that sought to find different forms of expression for a new kind of awareness. In Barcelona this was called modernisme, in Britain and the USA it was known as the Modern Style, in Vienna it was Secession, in Paris and Brussels it was described as art nouveau, and in German, *Jugendstil.* Interest in art nouveau/art deco has grown in recent years, and has especially focussed on objects of practical use. Initially less thought was given to architecture. Major architects of the period include Victor Horta, Henry van de Velde and Paul Hankar, who together made Brussels a veritable treasure chest of the Arts Décoratifs. To be sure, not much remains, as so many buildings have been demolished. But now restoration work is being carried out. The most interesting art nouveau buildings are to be found in the Quartiers St-Gilles and Ixelles, and for instance at the Place du Chatelein, where Karl Marx and Rodin lived. *The T.I.B. transport office organizes walking tours on these themes led by trained city guides.*

IMPORTANT BUILDINGS & MONUMENTS

Albertine **(108/A4)**
The Mont des Arts is something of a showpiece, being the site of the royal library, *Bibliothèque Albert I*, together with the Palais des Congrès and the Palais de la Dynastie. These facilities date from the years 1956–1958. The statue of King Albert I on horseback, the gardens and the broad flight of steps are impressive in their simplicity. From here there is a fine view of the city centre. The library is well stocked, with more than a million volumes, as well as manuscripts and historical works. *Open Mon–Fri 9 am–8 pm, Sat 9 am–5 pm, Mont des Arts, Metro: Gare Centrale*

Atomium **(100/C3)**
Brussels' famous landmark commemorates the world exhibition of 1958. The Atomium symbolizes the structure of an iron crystal molecule magnified 165 billion times. The structure is 102 m high, and comprises nine spheres, each with a diameter of 18 m, connected together by large tubes containing escalators, to form a crystal lattice arrangement. The topmost sphere houses a restaurant with a panoramic view of Brussels, whilst the others house *Biogénium*, an exhibition of the history of medicine, immunology, genetics and virology. *Admission Bfr 200, Open daily Apr–Aug 9 am–8 pm, Sep–Mar 10 am–6 pm, Heysel, Metro: Heysel, Tram 23, 81*

Berlaymont **(109/D4)**
Up to 1992 this cross-shaped

glass palace was the European Union's administration building, and the EU Commission also met here. On the other side of Robert Schuman Square, the gigantic new EU Parliament building is growing taller and taller. Berlaymont was designed by de Vestel and built between 1963 and 1969 and rented out to the EU by the Belgium State. It eventually became too small for the growing numbers of bureaucrats and since 1992 it has been closed and is undergoing reconstruction, as the rooms were insulated with asbestos. The "Berlaymonster" is bureaucracy personified, only 40% of it ever having actually been used as offices. *Rond-Point-Schuman, Metro: Schuman*

Bourse **(107/E3)**
The Stock Exchange was built in neo-classical style by Léon Suys in 1873, right in the centre of the city. It has a fine classical portal

MARCO POLO SELECTION: SIGHTSEEING

1 **Galeries Saint-Hubert**
For 150 years the most elegant and exclusive shopping arcade in the city (page 18)

2 **Grand' Place**
The most beautiful market place in the world, a constant reminder of Brussels' glorious past (page 28)

3 **Sablon**
A magnet for people with taste and money. The *Place du Grand Sablon* is the centre of the antiques trade (page 30)

4 **Quartier des Marolles**
This "forgotten" district of Brussels in the very heart of the city provided Pieter Bruegel with inspiration for his paintings (page 31)

5 **Metro**
The underground stations of Brussels provide a cultural experience that is unique in Europe (page 25)

6 **Palais de Justice**
This colossal edifice on the Galgenberg, once the site of the city gallows, is even bigger than St. Peter's in Rome (page 20)

7 **Saint-Michel**
Brussels' cathedral is a most beautiful, richly carved Gothic building (page 23)

8 **Parc de Laeken**
The King of Belgium has his classical castle in the middle of this wooded parkland (page 28)

9 **Place des Martyrs**
The "Martyrs' Square", formerly an architectural gem, is the seat of the Flemish Government (page 30)

10 **Grimbergen**
A picture-book monastery with some of Belgium's most impressive baroque architecture (page 33)

with six Corinthian columns flanked by two lions. The pediment has a relief depicting "upright" Belgium. On the left, the archaeological museum *Bruxella 1238* has medieval objects on display *(guided tours Mon, Tue, Thu and Fri 10 am–12.30 pm and 1.30 pm–4 pm, admission Bfr 80)* Nearby are several pavement cafés, including the *Cirio* on the left and the *Falstaff* on the right. *Place de la Bourse, Metro: Bourse*

Founded in 1801, the Brussels Stock Exchange is the most important in Belgium

Colonne du Congrès (108/B3)
The 47 m high Congress Column, erected in 1850, commemorates the national congress of 1831, at which the Belgian Constitution was drawn up. A statue of King Leopold I adorns the top of the column, whilst the eternal flame in honour of the unknown soldier of the two World Wars burns at its foot. The square on which the column stands commands a fine panoramic view of the lower city. *Place du Congrès, tram: 92, 93, 94*

Galeries Saint-Hubert (107/E3)
★ These covered galleries, opened in 1847 were amongst the first shopping arcades in Europe. About 200 m long, they are divided into the Galerie du Roi ("King's Gallery"), Galerie des Princes ("Princes' Gallery") and Galerie de la Reine ("Queen's Gallery"). The walkways are lined with exclusive shops, cafés and a cinema. If you want to sit and watch the world go by, there are plenty of cafés and restaurants to choose from. The glass roof of the gallery provided the inspiration for Milan's Galleria Vittorio Emanuele. Juliette Drouet, Victor Hugo's mistress, lived in the Prince's Gallery in 1851. *Between rue de l'Ecuyer and Marché-aux-Herbes: Gare Centrale*

Manneken Pis (107/E4)
Most visitors are a bit disappointed when they see the famous "Manneken" for the first time, having imagined it to be considerably bigger. This "piddling" statue (in both senses of the word!) was commissioned by the magistrate Jérôme Duquesnoy in 1619. Known affectionately as *petit Julien,* or little Julius, it symbolizes the irreverent side of Brussels, and was just an ordinary fountain before it became the much-photographed emblem of the city. The Elector of Bavaria, Max Emanuel was the first to present the Manneken Pis with a uniform in 1698. Since then, such gifts have proliferated and the resulting collection of 600

King Baudouin's writing desk can be seen in the Palais Royal

garments can be viewed in the Broodhuis (Maison du Roi). *Rue de l'Etuve, Metro: Bourse*

Old England (108/A4)
At the Montagne de la Cour, the former department store Old England is particularly eye-catching. A whimsical and extremely fragile-looking construction of steel and glass with high windows, shimmering black and gold, Old England was built by the art nouveau architect Paul Saintenoy. The edifice is used for art exhibitions and will shortly become the home of the Museum of Musical Instruments when the roof café will also be open. *Rue Montagne de la Cour, Metro: Gare Centrale*

Palais des Beaux-Arts (108/A4)
The palace of fine arts was built in art deco style by the architect Victor Horta, proponent of that style in Belgium. The entrance on the *rue du Baron Horta* leads into the film museum and the cultural centre also contains many magnificent halls, the Salle Henry Le Boeuf being especially famous for its acoustics. *Rue Ravenstein 23, Metro: Gare Centrale*

Palais d'Egmont (107/F5)
This city palace, which now houses the Foreign Ministry was built for the Dukes of Arenberg in the 16th century. Famous people of that era who stayed here include Queen Christine of Sweden, Louis XV, Rousseau and Voltaire. The broad marble staircase in the right wing was modelled on the ambassador's staircase at Versailles. Behind the palace is a garden, part of which is open to the public, and in front a small park, *Petit Sablon,* extends to the *rue de la Régence.* The park was laid out in 1890, with 48 bronze statues symbolizing the guilds of Brussels, and others portraying the humanists Mercator and Dodenius as well as Count Egmont and Count Hoorne, who were beheaded on the Grand' Place in 1568, allegedly for plotting against the Spanish. *Petit Sablon 8, tram: 92, 93, 94*

Palais de Justice **(107/E6)**
★ The imposing law courts building dominates the whole city. At the time when it was built, it was the largest monumental building in Europe, and, situated up on the former gallows hill, it towers above the Marolles district. The architect Joseph Poelaert began the building in 1866, but died in 1879, four years before the work was completed. The Palais de Justice is more than one-third bigger than St Peter's in Rome, and houses 34 law courts, 245 large offices, eight libraries and 80 archives. It cost over 10 million Belgian francs when it was built, which would be much more today. From the *Place Poelaert* in front of the building there is an impressive view over the Marolles district. The entrance hall makes an excellent meeting place. *Metro: Louise*

Palais de la Nation **(108/B4)**
The French architect Barnabé Guimard built this classical-style palace for the Supreme Council of Brabant in 1783. After 1830 it became the national palace, where the representatives and the Senate meet. The building is open to the public on days when no meetings are being held. *Rue de la Loi 16, Metro: Parc, tram: 92, 93, 94*

Palais Royal **(108/B4)**
When the Belgian flag is flying over the royal palace, this is a sure sign that King Albert II is in residence. Throughout history the palace, which has always been the home of influential families, has played an important role, starting in the early Middle Ages, with the Dukes of Brabant, who lived in the old palace on the Coudenberg. Jacoba of Bavaria fled from the palace to get away from Duke Jan IV. The Dukes of Burgundy, the Habsburg emperors, and later the princes of the Renaissance all lived here. In 1520, Albrecht Dürer described the palace, with its fountains, maze, and animal gardens, as the nearest thing he had ever seen to Paradise. And later, Emperor Charles V said it was "a truly royal palace, so large, that there is room for the emperor, the princes, the queens and ladies of the court and all the officers."

At that time Brussels must have been truly an architectural gem, set in a beautiful landscape of hills and woods, rivers and islands. From the hill on which the palace stands, the inhabitants had a beautiful view over the old town and the Grand' Place (or "Grote Markt" as it is known in Flemish). But this happy state of affairs was not to last. In 1731 the palace was completely destroyed by fire. Under French rule Brussels went into a decline, ending up merely as a base for the Prefect van de Dyle. Even under the new dynasty under King William I of Holland (after 1815), reconstruction of the palace only took place in a half-hearted way, for reasons of economy. It was not until the Counts of Saxe Coburg arrived that a new palace was built in neoclassical style. It was completed under Leopold II, and the façade, in the style of Louis XVI was added in 1904.

The interior cannot fail to impress, simply by virtue of its

In the spirit of Marco Polo

Marco Polo was the first true world traveller. He travelled with peaceful intentions forging links between the East and the West. His aim was to discover the world and explore different cultures and environments without changing or disrupting them. He is an excellent role model for the travellers of today and the future. Wherever we travel we should show respect for other peoples and the natural world.

WWF

enormous size, quite apart from its marble in many colours, its fine parquet floors, expensive types of wood, chandeliers of all sizes and lavish use of gold paint. The *Hôtel de Bellevue*, situated on the west side, is open to the public as a branch of the royal museum for history and art. *Open July–Sep, Tue–Sun 10.30 am–4.30 pm for viewing of the inner rooms of the palace; daily at 2.30 pm changing of the guard, admission free, Place des Palais, Metro: Trône, tram: 92, 93, 94*

Porte de Hal (111/D2)

The *Porte de Hal* or *Hallepoort* is Brussels' last remaining city gate. This fortified tower, which dates from the 14th century, now houses the folk museum. *Open Tue–Sat 10 am–5 pm, admission Bfr 150, Avenue de la Porte de Hal, Metro: Porte de Hal*

Théâtre Royal de la Monnaie (107/E3)

The national opera takes its name from the former mint building which was pulled down in 1531. The first theatre was built in 1698, and the new theatre was opened in 1819. The latter building was the scene of the unforgettable historical events that took place on 25 August 1830. At the première of the opera "The Voice of Portici", after the song "To Arms" had rung out, the audience, together with other residents of Brussels who were waiting outside, stormed the houses inhabited by the occupying powers. This marked the beginning of the Belgians' fight for freedom against the unpopular occupation by Holland. In 1855 the building was destroyed by fire.

The present beautiful neoclassical building with the colonnaded portico, which was preserved, has been renovated at great expense. The entrance hall, with its black and white floor mosaic was designed by the American architect Sol Lewitt, and the ceiling triptych was painted by his compatriot Sam Francis. The auditorium retains all its old magnificence and splendour, and so does the royal box. *Tickets: Tel. 229 12 11, Place de la Monnaie, Metro: De Brouckère*

CEMETERY

(103/F1) Bordering on *Laeken* is "God's acre". Between the main entrance and the church of *Notre-Dame de Laeken*, built in the 19th

The cemetery at Laeken with "The Thinker" by Rodin

century, flickers the flame commemorating the Belgian soldiers who lost their lives in the North Africa campaign. The cemetery is a stone city of the dead, consisting of chapels, sarcophagi, marble crosses and statues. Figures of angels mourn dead generals, artists and citizens. King Albert I and King Baudouin also lie buried in the royal crypt. Tombs of particular interest include that of the artist Jef Dillen, watched over by a copy of Auguste Rodin's famous statue "The Thinker". *Open Tue–Sun, Parvis Notre-Dame de Laeken, Metro: Bockstael, Tram 81, 94*

CHURCHES

Basilique Nationale du Sacré-Cœur (102/A4)

The people of Brussels refer to their church of the Sacred Heart as the "Basilica of the Koekelberg". It took more than fifty years to complete this art-nouveau-style edifice. The work was started in 1905, and throughout the long building period several changes were made to its architectural style. *(Open daily 8 am–6 pm in summer)* Beautiful view from the dome. *(Open Easter–October daily 8 am–6 pm, Nov–Easter daily 8 am–5 pm, admission Bfr 100) Koekelberg, Metro: Simonis*

Notre-Dame de la Chapelle (107/E5)

The "chapel church", on the edge of the Marolles district, is so called because it occupies the site of a Romanesque chapel. This is the last resting place of the painter Pieter Bruegel, who is buried with his wife Maria Coucke in a side chapel. The present Gothic church was built between 1421 and 1483, with the baroque tower being completed in 1599. A striking feature is the grimacing faces which adorn the façade. Restoration work on this very ancient church, whose original foundation stone was laid in

1134, has now been completed. *Open June–Sep 9 am–5 pm, Sat 1.30 pm–5 pm, Sun 1.30 –3.30 pm, Place de la Chapelle, tram: 92, 93, 94*

Notre-Dame du Sablon (107/F5)
On the boundary between the Place du Petit-Sablon and the Place du Grand-Sablon stands the church of Notre-Dame du Sablon. This large late Gothic building, whose main central nave is flanked by a double aisle on both sides, was the church of the guild of crossbow-men, who had their exercise ground here on the sand (*sablon* or *zavel*). The church was built in the 15th century and is famous for having a miracle-working statue of the Madonna. *Open daily 9 am–5.30 pm, rue de la Régence, tram 92, 93, 94*

Sainte-Catherine (107/D–E3)
The church of St Catherine, not far from the Stock Exchange, dominates the Fish Market. The church, currently being restored, dates back to the 14th and 15th centuries. The present three-aisled building was built in a mixture of Gothic and Renaissance styles by the architect Joseph Poelaert in 1854, having practically fallen into ruin by the beginning of the nineteenth century. Amongst the church's treasures is a black Madonna dating from the 14th century, which is especially interesting. *Open Mon–Sat 8.30 am–6 pm, Place Ste Catherine, Metro: Ste Catherine*

Saint-Jean-Baptiste au Béguinage (107/E2)
The church of the Béguinage is an outstanding example of Flemish-Italianate baroque architec-

The Basilique Nationale du Sacré-Cœur

ture. It is built on the site of a Béguinage, a community of lay sisters *(béguines)* who lived as nuns, but took no vows and were free to return to the world. Currently being restored, the church is impressively spacious. Outstanding features include its carved wooden confessionals, the choir, the immense wooden pulpit and numerous paintings including works by Van Loon, a native of Brussels and contemporary of the architect Fayd' Herbe, to whose plans the church was built between 1657 and 1676. *Open Tue 10 am–5 pm, Wed–Fri 9 am–5 pm, Sun 9.30 am–1.30 pm, Place du Béguinage, Metre: Ste-Catherine*

Saint-Michel (107/F3)
★ St Michael's Cathedral stands impressively on the slope between the lower city and upper city. This is Brussels' main church and houses many works of art. Restoration work on the façade, which has taken many

years, has now finally been completed and the building positively glows. The immense edifice was constructed in the 13th to 15th centuries in the Gothic style of Brabant. The choir is Romanesque, the nave early Gothic, and its solid twin towers are in Flemish Gothic style. The church has an abundance of stained glass, some of it in leaded windows dating back as far as the 16th century. The windows in the choir depict rulers from Flemish history, whilst those in the transept show Charles V with his wife, and his brother-in-law Louis II with his wife Maria. The choir, an impressive example of high Gothic style,

St Michael's cathedral, where Belgium's kings are crowned

contains memorials to Duke Jan II of Brabant and Archduke Albrecht. To the left of the choir, and also in Gothic style, is a chapel dedicated to Notre-Dame de la Délivrance. The 17th century windows are by a pupil of Rubens. The wood-carved pulpit dates from 1699, a beautiful example of Belgian baroque showing Adam and Eve being driven out of Paradise. *Open daily 8 am–6 pm, crypt: admission Bfr 40, Place Ste-Gudule, Metro: Gare Centrale*

Saint-Nicolas (107/E3)
This modest church is one of Brussels' most popular places of worship and its history is closely bound up with that of the city. It stands on Romanesque foundations, was built in Gothic style during the 14th and 15th centuries, then destroyed in the French bombardment of 1695 and rebuilt in the original style. Today it is hidden away behind houses which obscure its fine external front. The church possesses a large treasury and its fine furnishings, wood-panelled walls and confessionals are particularly impressive. It has a 17th century portrayal of Mary and a 16th century depiction of Christ. *Open daily 7.45 am–6.45pm, rue au Beurre, Metro: Bourse*

METRO

★ The Metro stations of Brussels are museums that are visited by approximately 450,000 people daily. The idea of this underground museum of modern art arose when the underground system was built in 1965. The architects who had been commissioned with the planning had the brilliant idea of getting the country's artists to design the underground stations. Over the course of time these museum stations have come into being, unique in Europe – apart from the example of Stockholm, where the idea has not been implemented so consistently. In Brussels "Art in the Metro" has now become an institution, with folding plans, books and organized tours. Over the years works of art have been produced in glass and ceramics, figures have been set up, wall-tapestries woven, and sculptures created in bronze, steel and wood. Examples include Hilde von Sumere's Carrara marble sculpture at Osseghem and Paul Delvaux's *Nos Vieux Trams Bruxellois* at the Bourse station. The station in Aumale is covered with huge photos showing how the city looked before the underground was constructed: a work of art that Jean-Paul Laenen created in 1982, entitled *Metrorama 78*. Comic-strip pictures of Tintin are painted on the wall at Bockstael, Paul de Gobert created the landscape at Vandervelde Station, and the Station Botanique is dominated by the 21 large figures *Les Voyageurs. One-day ticket Bfr 130, ten-journey booklet Bfr 330, information T.I.B. transport office, Hôtel de Ville*

PARKS & GARDENS

Bois de la Cambre (U/C5)
⊙ It is generally agreed that the city's most beautiful park is Ter Kameren, the *Bois de la Cambre* park, laid out as a centre for recreation. The park occupies 108

ha of slightly hilly landscape with a lake (boat hire), playing fields, riding stables and a running and walking path that leads over into the large forest of Soignes. The adjacent Avenue Franklin D. Roosevelt is flanked by embassy buildings, old villas and lecture halls of the old university. At the end of Avenue Louise stands the Cistercian abbey *La Cambre*, whose church dates back to the 14th to 16th centuries. The abbey buildings are classical 18th century. To the west of Avenue Louise stands the *Museum Constantin Meunier*, attached to the painter's former home and studio, which are open to the public. *Tram: 23, 90,93*

Bruparck (100/C3)

Bruparck is made up of four leisure centres: the cinema multiplex *Kinépolis*, the swimming paradise *Oceadium*, a layout of famous European landmarks in miniature *Mini-Europe* and a model Brabant village *Le Village.*

Kinépolis: With 26 auditoriums seating a total of 4,500 people, this is the largest cinema complex in the world. Apart from its sheer size, its special attraction lies in the fact that the films are projected on to a screen measuring 600 sq m. *Programme information and admission prices: Tel. 474 26 00 and 0900/005 55, Boulevard du Centenaire 1, Metro: Heysel, by car: Brussels Ring, Exit No. 8 Wemmel-Heysel.*

Mini-Europe: Three hundred buildings from EU countries, including historical city centres (Antwerp), architectural monuments (the leaning tower of Pisa, the Holsten Tower, Big Ben, and the Acropolis of Athens) have been constructed on a 1:25 scale on a site occupying 2.5 ha. There are also port installations, an airport, the Ariane Rocket and the Berlin Wall, which collapses at the push of a button!
Open Mar–beginning Jan, daily 9.30 am–6.30 pm, admission Bfr 395, children Bfr 295, Tel. 474 13 13

Oceadium: This tropical swimming paradise, occupying an area of 7,000 square metres, is designed to make visitors feel as if they are on holiday under the palm trees. There are saunas, a swimming pool with a wave machine, and flumes. *Open daily 10 am–8 pm, admission from Bfr 460, Tel. 478 43 20*

Le Village: Behind the village's historic façades you will find restaurants, snack bars, pubs, souvenir shops and boutiques.

Jardin Botanique (108/A–B2)

This French-style garden is closed in by busy streets. At its centre the former grandiose hothouses now house the cultural centre of the French-speaking inhabitants of Brussels, with exhibition halls, a theatre, cinema and an attractive, intimate café. *Rue Royale, Metro: Botanique*

Parc de Bruxelles (108/A–B4)

Brussels' beautiful city park, between the royal palace and the national palace, was laid out by the Dukes of Brabant as a game reserve in the 15th century, with lakes, grottoes and woods. It lies between the Royal Palace and the Palace of the Nations.

In 1830 this was the scene of the first fighting between Dutch troops and Belgian patriots. At the end of the 18th century the park, which forms part of the architectural work of art, known as *Warande*, by the landscape gardener Zinner, was transformed in accordance with French geometric garden designs. A beautiful fountain plays at the centre, and many nameless statues by native artists are distributed throughout the park. *Concerts are held here in summer.* The royal park theatre, *Théâtre Royale du Parc*, an intimate playhouse can be found at the corner of the park between *rue de la Loie* and *rue Ducale, Metro: Trône, Parc*

Parc Duden **(110/B–C5)**
In the south of the suburb of Forest lies the Duden park, named after a German industrialist. Occupying 23 hectares of park and woodland this was the hunting ground of Emperor Charles V in the 16th century. *Forest, tram: 18, 55, bus: 48, 50, 54*

King Leopold II's hothouses swallowed up a fortune

Parc de Laeken (101/D–F4)

★ ⊙ The royal estate of Laeken is one of the city's enclosed areas of park and woodland. At the centre is the residence of the royal family, built in classical style between 1782 and 1784 for the governor Duke Albert of Saxony. In the park is the most beautiful and largest hothouse of the *belle époque*, known as the "glass city", which has been handed down to posterity by King Leopold II. The king, who directed the creation of his gardens for 25 years, ordered the plants from a catalogue and invested enormous sums of money in exotic species. He is said to have personally overseen the day-to-day operations in the 36 hothouses. The plants have been especially selected to bloom from early spring to late autumn, with colours changing from light to dark. A path approximately 700 m long connects the various parts of the glass city to each other, and provides a walkway under glass, through hundreds of thousands of flowers and blossoms, producing an atmosphere of fragrance, colour and light. The plants here, in what is perhaps the most beautiful botanical garden in the world, are all housed indoors, in a space just two kilometres long – an area of two hectares under four hectares of glass.

The climax of the glass city is the conservatory built in 1876 and designed by the art nouveau architect Alphonse Balat. This is in the form of a rotunda measuring 57 m across, with a dome reaching a height of 25 m, resting on 36 Doric columns. On a hill in front of the residence (which is not open to the public) the monument to Leopold I. commands a magnificent view over Brussels. At the northern edge of the garden stand the Chinese pavilion and the Japanese tower. *Open Tue–Sun 10–4.45 pm. The hothouses are open for a few days once a year at the end of Apr/beginning of May. Information Tel. 513 89 40, tram: 52, 92, bus: 53*

SQUARES

De Brouckère (107/E3)

Along one side of this square runs the *Boulevard Adolphe-Max* which, with the historic passage *Du Nord* and the *Boulevard Anspach*, make up the most mercurial part of the city. In the evening especially, the neon advertising signs, give the impression of a true metropolis. The last remaining buildings of the *belle époque* are now being restored. *Metro: De Brouckère.*

Grand' Place (107/E4)

★ The Grand' Place well deserves its world-wide reputation as a famous and popular market place. A confusion of narrow streets lead off the square, which is almost perfectly rectangular, into the old town. The architecture of the guildhalls is a blend of late Gothic, Baroque and Renaissance. The present square, which is about 110 m long and 70 m wide, and free of cars, is in fact a reconstruction of the medieval square which, on 13th and 14th August 1695 was bombarded by the French Marshal de Villeroy on the orders of King Louis XIV, and went up in flames together with a further 4,000 houses in the city centre. The reconstruction of the city was completed in record time, taking only eight years, this time being built in stone with baroque façades in the Flemish-Italianate style which was fashionable at the time, with special attention being paid to the decorative gables. The construction work was directed by the city's powerful guilds, such as the brewers, bakers, butchers, cabinet-makers and joiners.

Le Roi d'Espagne, Nos. 1 and 2, is the Bakers' Hall. On the façade of this building is a portrait of King Charles II of Spain, with two black prisoners. The ornate gable is topped by an outstanding octagonal cupola with a golden statue.

La Brouette, No. 3, was the guildhall of the tallow makers, built in Flemish Renaissance style in 1697. Here you can see a niche containing a statue of the guild's patron saint, St Gilles.

Le Sac, No. 4, is the guildhall of the coopers and cabinet makers.

La Louvre, No. 5, in Italianate-Flemish style, is the archers' building. It is known as the "She-Wolf" because of the relief sculpture above the doorway.

Le Cornet, No. 6, is the boatmen's guildhall, and the second floor of the façade has some nautical features. "Le Cornet" means the "horn of plenty".

Le Renard, No. 7, ("the fox"), was the haberdashers' guildhall. The façade is especially beautiful, with its five statues: in the centre is the figure of Justice, and at her sides symbolic represenatations of the four continents which had been discovered at that time. The building is surmounted by a statue of the guild's patron saint, St Nicholas.

L'Étoile, No. 8, ("the star"), was the jurors' meeting place. It was pulled down in 1852 and rebuilt in 1897.

Le Cynee, No. 9, ("the swan") was the butchers' guildhall. Karl Marx and Friedrich Engels met here and this is where the Belgium trade union movement was born.

L'Arbre d'Or, No. 10, (the "golden tree"), is still the official headquarters of the brewing association.

La Rose, No. 11, and *Le Mont Thabor, No. 12* were the homes of private citizens.

The end wall of the Grand' Place is taken up by the *Maison des Ducs de Brabant*, which consists of six buildings. Restoration work on this "house of the Dukes of Brabant" was finally completed in 1991 since when the gold leaf has shone brilliantly in the sun.

Numbers 20 to 23, Cerf Volant ("flying stag"), *Joseph et Anne* and *L'Ange* ("the angel") were private houses. The tailors' guild owned *La Chaloupe d'Or* ("the golden boat") and *La Taupe* ("the mole").

Le Pigeon, Nos. 26 and 27, was the painters' guildhall; the French writer Victor Hugo lived here in 1852 during his period of exile in Brussels, during which time he wrote part of his cycle *Les Contemplations.*

Numbers 34–39 adjoin the *Maison du Roi* (the "King's House"). These six buildings form a kind of architectural unity, as each floor retains the same threefold arrangement of columns. The houses, whose façades are typical examples of Flemish baroque, are named *Le Heaume* ("the helmet"), *Le Paon* ("the peacock"), *Le Petit Renard* ("the little fox"), *Le Chêne* ("the oak"), *Ste-Barbe* and finally *No. 39 L'Âne* ("the donkey").

The most striking building on the Grand' Place is the City Hall, which is a Gothic masterpiece. Its architects included Jan van Ruysbroeck and Jacob van Thienen. The Gothic spire is topped by a 5 m high weather vane dating from 1455, which represents the Archangel Michael who is the patron saint of the city. Countless renovations and additions have been carried out, and the town hall finally acquired its present appearance in the second half of the nineteenth century. The two fountains in the inner court symbolize the rivers Maas and Schelde; whilst inside the building a rich collection of art includes 16th century wall tapestries and 18th century paintings. *Tours: 1 Apr–30 Sep, Sun and Tue 10 am, admission Bfr 80, Metro: Gare Centrale, bus: 63, 65, 66, 71*

Place des Martyrs (107/F2)

★ This is one of the city's most beautiful squares. It is surrounded by imposing houses which were inhabited by Brussels' more prosperous citizens right up the 1960s. The square itself, with its harmonious, rectangular layout, dates from 1774/75. The classical façades were allowed to decay until well into the 1990s. Now at last restoration is being carried out. One complex is already being used by the Flemish government, whilst other buildings are being converted into flats. The monument in the middle of the square commemorates the uprising against the Dutch in 1830: 467 "martyrs" of that revolution lie in the tomb. Their names are listed on the marble panels around the walls, whilst above, the lion "Belgium" bursts its chains. *Metro: Rogier*

Sablon (107/E5)

★ For antique-lovers with money to spend, this is most definitely the place to go. The *Place du Grand-Sablon* is the centre of Brussels' antiques trade, and an antiques market is held here every weekend. This is where expensive and often valuable items regularly change hands: second-hand tools, old lace, paintings, furniture, glasses. Around the market there are a host of cafés, restaurants, patisseries and antique shops. The *Au Pain Quotidien* at No. 11 serves breakfast and delicious snacks, and also has a garden. *(Open daily 7 am–7 pm).*

The trapeze shaped and gently sloping square is bordered by many fine mansions, and the church which lies across it separates the *Place du Grand-Sablon* from the *Place du Petit-Sablon*, a small square with formal gardens. *Tram: 92, 93, 94*

DISTRICTS OF THE CITY

Quartier Fontainas (110/C1–2)

An especially quiet district which is situated on high ground in the triangle between the station *Gare du Midi*, and the *Avenue de la Porte de Hal*. Here the streets follow a regular pattern. The population is mixed, with some foreigners, some old-established citizens and a number of young people; the district gets very lively and noisy as you go towards the area around the station, the Gare du Midi. The Cité Fontainas, once inhabited by retired teachers, has now been converted to provide social housing. *Metro: Porte de Hal*

Quartier Léopold (108–109/C–D5)
Once a popular and refined residential area, with numerous luxurious mansions. The district was built up in the 19th century. It lies between *rue de la Loi* and *rue du Trône* and is crossed by the *rue du Luxembourg*. Many buildings have been destroyed, although the *Place Frère-Orban* still has several beautiful houses. Towering up behind the station façade, on which there is a preservation order, are the enormous glass palace of the European Parliament building and the Congress Building, which also overshadow the ancient buildings in the Parc Léopold, which was once laid out as a zoo. *Metro: Trône, Arts-Loi*

Quartier des Marolles (107/D–E4–5)
★ ⊛ It is a long time since the natives of Brussels regarded the Marolles district as a well-kept secret. Unlike the Grand' Place or the Mont des Arts, the *Quartier des Marolles* scarcely gets a mention in the guidebooks. In this part of the city, around the *Vossenplein*, live craftsmen, petty criminals, the lower middle classes, immigrants and those whom life seems to have passed by. Washing is hung out from the windows, in the shops the fruit is arranged artistically, the vegetables displayed symmetrically, and the smell of burnt oil emanates from countless chip pans.

The boundary between the *Quartier des Marolles* and the neighbouring middle-class district runs between the *rue des Minimes* and the *Avenue de la Porte de Hal*, with the impressive 14th century tower to the *Avenue de Stalingrad*. In between, amidst grey tiled roofs and sparkling towers lies the ⚲ *Place du Jeu de Balle. A flea market is held here every day, including Sunday.* This square, the Flemish name of which is *Vossenplein*, has been a marketplace since 1873. People jostle their way through the Sunday drizzle, buyers and sellers liven up the street bazaar: men and women in Middle-Eastern dress, Arabs and Jews; children crowding their mothers, fathers browsing amongst refrigerators and televisions. With luck you may find just the right chair, sofa or kitchen cupboard. There are picture frames and oil paintings. Here someone sits reading an Arab newspaper while music drones through the loudspeaker of a cassette player. A heady mixture of fragrances from herbs and perfumes is dominated by a strong scent of violet. And a colourful mixture customers, people from Spain, Portugal and France, nationalities who have lived here since the Middle Ages, browse among displays of second-hand tools, ink bottles, cooking pots, furs, china, coins, medals, weapons, maps, clothes or walking sticks. In recent years they have been joined by people from the Maghreb.

The district's population numbers about 10,000, of whom about one third are here illegally. As in the Middle Ages, the district, which seems to be in a constant state of decay, is once again a place of refuge for the persecuted, and the people here have developed a particular kind of social and sexual tolerance. Removed from any form of state control, they even speak their own dialect.

There are still the narrow

streets, the tiny houses with large families, the inhabitants, the Marolles themselves; they are people who speak their minds, who do not allow the police or the politicians to tell them what to do, and who have learned, over the centuries, that they cannot expect anything from the "powers that be", and that in the end they must learn to help themselves if they want to survive.

The flea market, with the adjacent shopping streets, the *rue Haute* and the *rue Blaes,* form the district's commercial centre. The former fire brigade barracks is held up as an example of successful restoration, with its elegant boutiques, expensive bookshops and exquisite antique shops. The flats in the building here are light and modern, but much too expensive for ordinary office workers. Unease also surrounds the increasing numbers of highly paid EU officials who are encroaching upon the district, awakening envy and arousing anger.

As long ago as the 13th century, the Marolles were regarded as disreputable, to the extent that a gallows was erected there; there were turnpikes and in 1628 the district was separated from the rest of the city by a wall. The people are renowned for their enjoyment of celebrations, and for their *joie de vivre.* The pictures of Pieter Bruegel the elder, most famous of all the Marolles, vividly depict their exuberance and sense of fun. Bruegel's gabled house, which has been renovated, is situated at *No. 132 rue Haute.* A memorial tablet pays tribute to this great Flemish art ist, who was a pupil of Hieronymus Bosch. The creator of the "Peasants' Dance" and "Peasants' Wedding" lies buried in the church *Notre-Dame de la Chapelle* at the edge of the district.

In this district, which is looked down upon by the middle classes, and where the word "architect" is still used today as a term of abuse, you will find plenty of simple cafés and restaurants, and if you are lucky, you may even find someone who will play you a tune on the accordion.

EXCURSIONS FROM BRUSSELS

Beersel **(U/B6)**

This small town is situated in the delightful Senne valley, no more than 10 km from the city centre. Beersel, (pop. 21,000) is famous for its long brewing tradition – Lambic and Gueuze, two well-known Belgian beers, are brewed here – and for its romantic moated castle, which was built around 1300 for the defence of Brussels. This striking building, with high towers at three of its corners, is made completely from bricks. It was in the possession of Emperor Charles V's chamberlain, has been inhabited by monks, and was finally used as a spinning mill. The museum has an exhibition of instruments of torture, and the town has some fairly basic pubs, where special beers are served with bread and cheese. *Tue–Sun 10 am–6 pm (Mar–Nov), from the Gare du Nord, by rail on the Halle line.*

Gaasbeek **(U/A5)**

The *Château de Gaasbeek*, 15 km west of Brussels is popular with visitors and natives alike. The estate of Gaasbeek has a very beautiful 40 ha park, landscaped in French style which is ideal for picnics. It originated in the 13th century, and was extended in the 16th. The castle was the home of Count Egmont, who was ultimately beheaded on the Grand' Place, allegedly for plotting against Spanish control, a fate which provided the inspiration for Goethe's play "Egmont". Nowadays the castle contains a museum with an extensive art collection. *Open Apr–Oct, Tue, Thu, Sat, Sun 10 am–5 pm, daily in July and Aug.*

Grimbergen **(U/C2)**
★ Grimbergen Abbey, 12 km outside Brussels, in the direction of Antwerp, is a real picture-book monastery, originally founded in 1130. In the 16th century the church was burnt out, and it was rebuilt in the 17th century. It is regarded as one of the most impressive works of Belgian baroque. The village, with its rustic buildings, lies in the delightful region of Pajottenland. The *coach house* (Koetshuis) has a *museum of rural life,* and the old water mill houses a *rustic café,* where you can sample the village's famous beer. *Sat–Sun, 2 pm–6 pm (1 Apr–30 Sep); Mira Observatory, Abdijstraat 20, Mon–Fri 2 pm–11 pm (closed July and Aug)*

The romantic castle in Beersel

Halle **(U/A6)**
Surrounded by an open, hilly landscape, 15 km from Brussels, Halle with its famous *St-Martins-Basilika* is a place of pilgrimage. Ever since the Middle Ages the faithful have been attracted to the 13th century black Madonna which can be seen above the high altar in the basilica. Legend has it that during a siege this wooden figure intercepted 32 canonballs. The town's inhabitants speak Flemish. *By train from Brussels (Gare du Nord)*

Nivelles **(O)**
The history of this small town, which lies about 30 km away from Brussels, is closely bound up with that of its monastery. Its main attraction is the collegiate *church of St Gertrude,* built in the 11th century and a fine example of the Romanesque style of the Rhineland. The church contains Carolingian and Merovingian remains. A market is held outside the church on Saturdays.

Wavre **(U/E-F6)**
Wavre lies 22 km from Brussels, and its main claim to fame is *Walibi,* the most famous and most-visited theme park in the country. It has more than 47 attractions, including the Sirocco (a big dipper which "loops the loop"), wild water rides, caves and animal shows, and the tropical swimming paradise "Aqualibi". *Walibi: Open beginning of Apr–beginning of Sep 10 am–6 pm, July–Aug 10 am–9 pm, Tel. 010/42 15 00 or 42 17 17, about 20 km from Brussels along the Brussels–Namur highway, Walibi exit.*

Two hours in a museum

The masterpieces of Bruegel, Rubens, Magritte and Ensor; the biggest comic museum in the world; art deco or modern art in the metro for the price of a ticket

With the Royal Museums of Art, the *Musées Royaux des Beaux-Arts de Belgique*, Brussels has one of the largest art collections in Europe. Up on the *Mont des Arts*, the "Arts Hill" that separates the upper city from the lower, the museums of old and modern art are closely connected. This, the most significant collection of art in the country, is of course only one of about 90 museums which can be found in Brussels, and typically reflects the creative genius for which the country has been famous for more than five hundred years. This city, where two cultures are interwoven, with creative artists and an open-minded public, as the capital of United Europe, is mindful of its cultural heritage and is in the process of organizing its treasures so that they can be displayed in an appropriate context. The numerous works of art were brought together from monasteries, by the Counts, by the Kings of Belgium, by steel barons and by prosperous citizens. Once Brussels became the capital of Belgium in 1830, a great deal of energy and enthusiasm went into building up the modern metropolis. Around the turn of the 19th/20th centuries the city was a centre of art nouveau and art deco, and supreme examples of these styles are now displayed in the Horta Museum. The multiplicity of museums is, in itself, highly impressive. The former Waucquez department store, built in the art nouveau style, now houses the world's largest Comic Museum. In the house where the Rotterdam humanist Erasmus lived and worked, you can gain an insight into the way of life led by well-to-do citizens around the year 1520, whilst the David and Alice van Buuren Villa, furnished in art deco style will give you an idea of how prosperous people lived at the beginning of the 20th century. In addition there is an extensive motor museum displaying the largest collection of vintage cars in Europe. Last, but not least, you

Brussels has everything, from old masters to comic strips

can admire the sumptuous collection of costumes belonging to the Manneken Pis in the Maison du Roi. Many museums arrange special exhibitions; information about these can be found in the events diary of the daily newspapers. A unique feature of Brussels is that Belgian artists have transformed its many Metro stations into galleries with sculptures, wall tapestries, paintings, mosaics, and much, much more.

Comic Museum **(107/F3)**
★★ The exciting history of the Belgian comic strip is documented in detail by the displays in this former ★ department store, completed by the art nouveau architect, Victor Horta, in 1906. In an area of 4,200 sq m under extensive glass roofs, the colourful figures from 25,000 comic strips spring to life and adventure in French, Dutch and English. The museum was

MARCO POLO SELECTION: MUSEUMS

1 Autoworld
It really is amazing what one individual can collect: 400 extremely valuable motor cars (page 40)

2 Comic Museum
Lucky, Quick and Flupke, Captain Haddock and lots more comic-strip heroes (page 36)

3 Maison d'Erasme
The home of the great Renaissance humanist, Erasmus, furnished in the style of the 16th and 17th centuries (page 37)

4 Musée Victor Horta
The stylish home of the famous art nouveau architect (page 39)

5 Musées Royaux des Beaux-Arts
The treasures of the kingdom, distributed over eight floors. Not to be missed (page 38)

6 Musée Royal de l'Armée et d'Histoire Militaire
An armoury of war, an important and extensive collection of miltary exhibits (page 41)

7 Musée Royal de l'Afrique Centrale
The most important museum devoted to colonial history in Africa (page 38)

8 Maison du Roi
Behind the façade of the "King's House" is where the colourful costume collection of Mannekin Pis is kept (page 37)

9 Waterloo
Re-enactments of the historical battle are staged here, on the very site where Napoleon Bonaparte was finally defeated (page 41)

10 Parc du Cinquantenaire
The "Jubilee Park" with its monumental triumphal arch bears witness to Belgium's glorious past (page 40)

opened in 1989, and its exhibitions include Tim and Struppi, the world of the Smurfs, Lucky and Moris, the father of Lucky Luke and a further 650 comic authors. Every year this comic treasury is visited by some 180,000 lovers of the "speech bubble". The *Brasserie Horta* serves Belgian specialities for about Bfr 320 (*Open 12 pm–3 pm, Sun until 4 pm).* Extensive library on comic themes, bookshop and souvenir shop. *Open Tue–Sun 10 am–6 pm, admission Bfr 200, rue des Sables 20, Tel. 219 19 80, Metro: Rogier, Botanique, bus: 38, 58, 61*

David et Alice Van Buuren (U/C5)
The van Buuren's villa provides a good opportunity for a trip out to the suburb of *Uccle*. The museum building, in art deco style, has an impressive collection of paintings from the 16th and 20th centuries, including an early version of the *Fall of Icarus* by Pieter Bruegel the Elder. An added attraction is the maze in the large gardens. The house was built in 1929 and has been a museum since 1973. *Open Sun 1 pm–5.30 pm, Mon 2–6 pm, admission Bfr 300, Avenue Léo Errera 41, Tel. 343 48 51, tram: 23, 90*

Institut Royal des Sciences Naturelles (109/C6)
The Royal Institute of Natural Sciences lies at the edge of the Leopold Park. Its main attractions include a dinosaur skeleton, the 20 m long skeleton of a blue whale, and a 135 million year old iguanadon skeleton. Other extensive collections cover the fields of geology, mineralogy, paleontology, zoology and anthropology. Exhibits also include sea creatures from the Arctic and Antarctic, insects and moon rock. *Open Tue–Sat 9.30 am–4.45 pm, Sun 9.30 am–6 pm, admission Bfr 150, Chaussée de Wavres 260, Metro: Trône, bus, 20, 34, 60, 80*

Maison d'Erasme (U/A-B4)
★ Erasmus's house in the suburb of *Anderlecht* has been renovated in its original style. This Flemish Gothic gabled house was the home of the humanist philosopher Erasmus of Rotterdam, and is where he wrote *Praise of Folly* in 1509. The house, which has been furnished in the style of that period, is not far from the collegiate church of Sts-Pierre-et-Guidon. Besides the philosopher's writing materials, exhibits include drawings by Dürer and Holbein, and archaeological finds. *Open daily except Tue and Fri 10 am–12 pm and 2 pm–5 pm, rue du Chapitre 31, Tel. 521 13 83, admission Bfr 50, Metro: St-Guidon, tram: 56, bus: 47, 49*

Maison des Brasseurs (107/E4)
The brewing museum, *Musée de Brasserie* is appropriately situated the cellar of *De Gouden Baum* (The Golden Tree), and there is an opportunity for sampling the beer at the end of the tour. *Admission Bfr 100, open daily 10 am–5 pm, Tel. 511 49 87, Grand' Place 10, Metro: Bourse, Gare Centrale*

Maison du Roi (107/E4)
★ The "King's House", along with the city hall, is one of the most impressive buildings on the Grand' Place. Rebuilt towards

the end of the 19th century, following the destruction of the old bakers' guildhall, the "*broodhuis*" (bread house) in 1695, it now houses the city museum. Besides numerous exhibits demonstrating the development of the city, the Gothic sculptures in the entrance and sculptural works from the 16th–18th centuries deserve special mention. One room is devoted entirely to the art of weaving wall hangings and tapestries, another to the Brussels school of painting of the 15th and 16th centuries. On the first and second floor the history and development of the city are well documented and this is also where you will find the costumes belonging to Brussels' famous Manneken Pis. More than 600 costumes which have adorned the tiny fountain figure over the course of the centuries are displayed here. He is said to have received his first garment, the blue traditional costume of the Elector of Bavaria, in 1698. *Open Mon–Fri 10 am–12.30 pm and 1.30 pm–5 pm, Sat and Sun 10 am–1 pm, admission Bfr 80, Grand' Place, Metro: Gare Centrale or Bourse, tram: 23, 52, 55, 81*

Musée de la Gueuze (U/A-B4)
One of Brussels' most original museums, the Gueuze Museum, which is situated in an old brewery, demonstrates the production process of typical Brussels beers such as Gueuze, Lambic or Kriek, which have to be drunk "fresh from the cellar" so to speak. *Open Mon–Fri 8.30 pm–5 pm, Sat 10 am–5 pm, admission Bfr 100, rue Gheude 56 (Anderlecht), Tel. 521 49 28, tram: 18, 23, 55, 90*

Musée Royal de l'Afrique Central (U/D-E4)
★☨ The Museum of Central Africa presents "white Belgian" colonialism. The museum, which resembles a castle, was opened by King Albert in 1910 and deals with this part of Belgian colonial history. The numerous rooms contain an extensive collection of masks and sculptures, preserved animals, birds and insects. An exhibition gives an insight into the life of natives in the former Belgian Congo, later to become Zaire. *Open Tue–Sun, 10 am–5 pm, public holidays 10 am–8 pm, admission Bfr 100, Chaussée de Louvain 13 (Tervuren), Tel. 769 52 11, tram: 44*

Musée Royaux des Beaux-Arts (108/A5)
The imposing park, with its large open-air flight of steps leading down to the city, came into being as the "Mont des Arts" ("Arts Hill") between 1956 and 1958 and lies between the *Place Royale*, the *Boulevard de l'Empereur* and the *Bibliothèque Albert I.* The wider complex also takes in the Royal Museums of Art, the ★ *Musée Royaux des Beaux-Arts de Belgique.* The treasuries of the Kingdom are regarded as unique. After a prolonged period of building activity the new underground building for the extensive "Modern Art" collection was opened in 1984. The galleries containing contemporary art are grouped around a semi-circular light shaft, 40 m wide. The *Palais Altenhoh,* also restored, which towers above this, houses the royal art collections.

It is well worth spending Bfr 20 on a *Museum Plan*, which will help you find your way around the extensive complex of galleries. It is of course impossible to see in one visit all 17,000 works of art, including 1,600 old masters, 2,660 19th century works and the Moderns, the numerous graphic works and engravings, as well as the sculptures, which are brought together in an exhibition area covering some 20,000 square metres. The exhibits are clearly arranged into categories taking in works from the 15th and 16th centuries, the 17th and 18th centuries and the 19th and 20th centuries. Current exhibitions have a room to themselves. The Ancient Art Museum is linked to the Modern Art Museum by means of an escalator. From the former museum, you come first to the rooms containing the early moderns, the Impressionists and Expressionists of the Latemse School – from the sunny paintings of Emiel Claus to the more sombre works of Permeke. The building also houses the most extensive collection of early Dutch and Flemish painting, including the Flemish "primitives". Important works include Hieronymus Bosch's *Calvary*, Hans Membling's *Martyrdom of St Sebastian* and Pieter Bruegel the Elder's famous *Fall of Icarus*. The Italian School is also represented, by Tintoretto, Tiepolo and Crespi, and there are also "old" German works, with the focus very much on Lucas Cranach. Views on the collection of modern art differ widely, but you should not miss seeing the works of James Ensor, a Belgian Expressionist from Ostend. Also recommended is are the Delvaux collection and the room devoted to René and George Magritte, where you can see three of the most important works of Belgian surrealism: *La magie noire*, *L'Empire des lumières* and *Le domaine d'Arnheim*. The collection of modern art of the 20th century also includes works by the Cobra Group and the Zero Group, with masterpieces by Max Ernst, Matisse, Gauguin and Dali. There is also a café and bookshop. *Open Tue–Sun 10 am–5 pm, admission Bfr 150, students and children Bfr 100, rue de la Régence 3, Tel. 508 32 11, tram: 92, 93, 94; bus: 20, 34, 38, 71, 60, 95, 96, Metro: Gare Centrale*

Musée Victor Horta **(111/E4)**

★ Whilst the museums of Brussels may justifiably be regarded as being amongst the most beautiful and greatest in Europe, the house built by the "Father" of Belgian art nouveau in 1898 is one of the most important – even though many guidebooks fail to even mention it. At the turn of the 19th/20th centuries, Victor Horta built many middle-class homes in this European style, and furnished them, but many have been demolished, whilst others are in private ownership and seldom open to the public, such as the *Haus Cauchie* or the *Hôtel Solvay* at *No. 224 Avenue Louise*. Horta was unable to furnish his own home and studio quite so luxuriously, but its architectural synthesis incorporates the very best elements of his period. *Open Tue–Sun 2 pm–5.30 pm, admission Bfr 150 (weekends Bfr 200), tours by arrangement, Tel. 543 04 90, rue Américaine 25 (St-Gilles), tram: 81, 82, 91, 92, bus: 54*

Palais des Beaux-Arts **(107/F4)**

The Palace of Fine Arts, built to

The Palais des Beaux-Arts

the plans of the art nouveau architect Victor Horta, regularly hosts events such as concerts, plays and conferences. This is not really a museum in the true sense of the word, but for anyone interested in the Belgian form of art nouveau, it is well worth a visit. The building houses the Cinema Museum, which shows silent films to piano accompaniment twice daily. *Open 5.30 pm–10 30 pm, admission Bfr 90, rue de Baron Horta 9, Tel. 507 83 70, Metro: Gare Centrale*

Parc du Cinquantenaire (109/E–F5)

★ The "Jubilee Park" was opened in 1880 to celebrate the fiftieth anniversary of the founding of the kingdom of Belgium. The triumphal arch, the *Arc du Cinquantenaire* with its bronze statue of a chariot drawn by four horses, can be seen from a considerable distance. The female figures at the foot of the three archways symbolize the Belgian provinces. To the left and right are colonnades, with representations of the history of Belgium. The monumental buildings on either side of the arch house the *Autoworld* museum, the Royal Collections of Art and History, the *Musées Royaux d'Art et d'Histoire,* and the Royal Army Museum, the *Musée Royal de l'Armée et d'Histoire Militaire.*

★ *Autoworld*. Not only car enthusiasts but many other visitors enjoy this fine exhibition. Since 1986 the former exhibition hall Palais Mondial has had an extensive, interesting and excellent display of motor cars. This magnificent collection of historical vehicles grew out of the private collection of the Mahy and De Pauw families. All the 400 cars on show, dating from between 1896 and 1979, are in working order. A "Walkman" can be hired, with English commentary, for Bfr 100. The museum's bookshop is entirely devoted to the subject of the motor car. Café. *Open daily 10 am–5 pm (Apr–Sep until 6 pm), admission Bfr 200, Tel. 736 41 65, tram: 81, Metro Merode*

Musées Royaux d'Art et d'Histoire. Before you even get inside this museum, you will be impressed by its magnificent structure of iron and glass. Built in 1880, its exhibits include precious finds from the age of antiquity, from the Middle Ages, from Asia and pre-Columbian South America. With its multiplicity of art treasures, this is one of the most famous museums of art and history in the world. The extensive collections are divided up into several large departments: European and Mediterranean cultures from early history to classical antiquity, then Belgian culture, Christian Europe, and the cultures of South

America and Asia. There is an enormous model of the city of Rome as it would have appeared in 400 B.C., and a colonnade from the Syrian city of Apamea. The museum's special treasures include the 16th century wall tapestries depicting the *Legend of Our Lady of Sablon*, the *Transfiguration* and the *Battle of Roncevaux* (Rooms 16–30). Special exhibitions are also held regularly. *Tue–Fri 9.30 am–5 pm, Sat–Sun 10 am–5 pm, admission Bfr 150, free guided tours by arrangement, Tel. 741 72 11, Metro: Merode, tram: 81 South wing of the Palais du Cinquantenaire.*

★ *Musée Royal de l'Armée et d'Histoire Militaire.* The museum illustrates the history of wars during the past three hundred years, up to the Second World War. It has an impressive collection of swords, canons, tanks and aircraft (Hurricane, Spitfire, Mosquito, Starfighter). The tanks and the air and space departments are amongst the most popular in the museum, and its armour collection, organized according to particular themes, which is regarded as the most important of its kind in Europe, also attracts many visitors. Displays explain what happened in many theatres of war, for example at the Battle of the Ardennes. *Open Tue–Sun 9 am–midday and 1 pm–4.45 pm, admission free, Tel. 734 52 52. Metro: Merode, tram: 81. North wing of the Palais du Cinquantenaire*

Waterloo **(U/C6)**

★ On 18 June 1815 the Prussians led by Blücher and the English led by Wellington defeated Napoleon's "Great Army". At the crossing point of the roads to Ohain and Charleroi, stand three memorials, commemorating this historical battle: the stone column, to the memory of Belgium's dead, the Hannoverians' monument and the memorial to Wellington's adjutant, who was killed in the battle. Every year Waterloo is visited by a million people. From the famous Lion Mound it is possible to see the whole battlefield, covering an area of two square kilometres, where 50,000 soldiers and 15,000 horses perished. The artificial, cone-shaped mound is 45 metres high, measures 500 metres across and has 226 steps leading up to the bronze lion. At the foot of the Lion Mound is a visitor centre, a round building where an antique panoramic picture of the battle can be seen. *Lion Mound, Panorama Museum: open daily 10.30 am–5 pm (Apr), 9.30 am–6.30 pm (May–Sep), 9.30 am–5 pm (Oct), 10.30 am–4 pm (Nov–Mar), admission Bfr 300, Route du Lion 252–54, Tel. 385 19 12*

Waxworks: Napoleon consulting his generals: Open Apr–Oct daily 9.30 am– 6.30 pm, Nov–Mar daily 10 am–5 pm, admission Bfr 60, Route du Lion 317

Wellington Museum: former inn, used by the Duke of Wellington as his command centre: Oct–Mar daily 10.30–5 pm, Apr–Oct daily 9.30–6.30 pm, admission Bfr 100, Chaussée de Bruxelles 147 (Waterloo Centre). This is also the tourist office with information about Waterloo, bus stop for the orange bus line W

Ferme de Caillou: Napoleon's Headquarters: Open Apr–Oct daily 9.30 am–7 pm, Nov–Mar daily 1.30 pm–5 pm, admission Bfr 60, Chaussée de Bruxelles 60

18 km south of Brussels, Bus line W from Place Rouppe; it takes a whole day to see everything

König
Pilsener
De Telegraaf
Teveel studiegeld sneller aflossen

Where to dine

Brussels is a gourmet's dream with 1,800 restaurants to suit every taste

In Brussels, art and cooking have gone hand in hand for centuries, as clearly shown by the paintings of the Flemish masters: the merry carousals, the colourful market scenes, the opulent banquets, the sweet-toothed cooks, and the still life paintings in which food and drink repeatedly play a prominent part. Pieter Bruegel's busy scenes of peasant life, Abel Grimmer's picture of *The Harvest*, Jacob Jordaen's bacchanalian painting of *The King Drinking* and Rubens' pictures of the Kirmes festival are bound to spring to mind, when you think about good food here in Brussels. The locals themselves have high expectations when it comes to eating out, and they are not often disappointed.

The fact that the city has some 1,800 restaurants and bistros testifies to the importance attached to gastronomy. The commercial and spiritual life of Brussels would be unimaginable without the opportunity to dine out in style, and to eat well at home on Sunday (which is why most good restaurants close on Sundays).

Eating is a serious matter, with 1,800 restaurants and bistros awaiting you

Mealtimes are an important part of life and play an indispensable part in the daily routine. Visitors, too, can enjoy this delight in good food.

The renowned restaurants are places where not only the representatives of the new EU élite – ministers, lobbyists, EU politicians, industrialists and top officials – but also successful artists meet to talk politics over their meal. Here the rule is not that you have to work, but that you have to interrupt work. After all, budgets, olive oil lakes and grain mountains can be discussed much better over a few well-cooked courses in a restaurant, than over a canteen meal. It is always a matter of luck whether your first encounter with the local gastronomy will be a positive experience. It is generally the case that bistros are more down to earth and have more atmosphere than the expensive restaurants, but they are also more crowded and chaotic.

With restaurants such as *Comme Chez Soi, La Truffe Noir, Bruneau,* and *Maison du Cygne,* haute cuisine is as well represented as are the mussel dishes of fine bistros such as *Léon* and *Ogenblick.* If you investigate the restaurants which have been awarded chef's hats, irises, spoons or stars, it is clear that no other European city of comparable size has so many excellent eating-houses. The "Michelin" guide alone has awarded its highest mark of distinction, three stars, to two restaurants. In addition there are almost half a dozen gourmet temples with two stars, and more than a dozen with one star. You really are spoilt for choice. But how do you find the right place to eat? Of course help is at hand, in the form of gourmet guides, the restaurants recommended here, and simply having a good "nose". A local wishing to visit a restaurant with which he is not familiar will bear the following rules in mind: be sceptical about any establishments whose doors are covered with all kinds of recommendation signs. Be sure to look at the menu. Are the prices what you would expect of this kind of restaurant? If a place is empty at mealtimes, be suspicious. Visitors also would do well to follow these guide lines. Caution is also recommended in the streets around the Grand' Place, where restaurant owners entice unsuspecting visitors with opulent window displays of fish and game. The majority of such

MARCO POLO SELECTION: RESTAURANTS

1 **Aux Armes de Bruxelles**
The waiters have class, the diners have class and so does the food (page 51)

2 **L'Etoile d'Or**
This is the last restaurant that still has a tiled stove (page 52)

3 **Café du Dôme**
Unusually low-calorie food served in art nouveau surroundings (page 52)

4 **Bonsoir Clara**
Fairly trendy, fairly good and extravagantly decorated (page 49)

5 **Claude Dupont**
A classic eating house popular with the gourmets of Brussels (page 50)

6 **L'Ogenblik**
The kind of bistro that anyone fond of eating out would like to have as his "local" (page 50)

7 **La Quincaillerie**
Food takes second place here as the beautiful waitresses steal the show (page 53)

8 **Au Stekerlapatte**
Full of atmosphere, comfortable and a good selection of substantial food (page 53)

9 **Halloween**
For those who like their meals to be spookily spectacular (page 52)

10 **Ultième Hallucinatie**
Here you can happily dine alone. Beautiful art nouveau décor (page 53)

Fresh displays of food delight the eye as well as the palate

establishments are unfortunately nothing but tourist traps.

The quality of Belgian cuisine can be attributed to the rich variety of regional cookery. A hot pot made with champagne has nothing in common with a *hutsepot* ("stew"). It is the product that gets all the attention, and the aim is not to bring "light meals" to the table. The art of Belgian cuisine is conservative and almost always potentially fatal to a slim figure. The strong attachment of the locals to the edible is even evident from the names of streets and squares. You can take a walk across the *rue Chair et Pain* ("Meat and Bread Street"), into the *Impasse des Groseilles* ("Redcurrant Alley"), along the *rue des Harengs* ("Herring Street"), stroll across the *rue du Marché aux Poulets* ("Chicken Market Street"), and end up in the *rue des Poissoniers* ("Fishmongers' Street") having worked up quite an appetite.

The bakers' shops sell *speculaas,* a kind of spiced biscuit, caramelised *pains à la Grecque,* (Brussels "canal bread"), *assekoeken* (round cakes) or *manos* made with whipped cream and nuts. Local produce includes Brabantine grapes, ripened in hothouses, hops in the spring, Brussel sprouts in winter and chicory, known as *witloof* in Flemish, all year round.

Fish is brought fresh from Ostend every day, and mussels, oysters and lobsters from Zeeland. There is plaice, turbot and tiny shellfish cooked in broth with celeriac. A *boestring* is a smoked herring, also used for Brussels omelette: the herrings are marinaded in milk, flaked

Nobody leaves the city without some of Brussels' world-famous, calorie-packed chocolates!

and cooked in a tomato and Madeira sauce, and served with the omelette. Other simple dishes are prepared with carp, cod and eel. These are traditionally accompanied by chips and beer. Brussels *hutsepot* is also famous, consisting of beef fried over a high heat with onions, then braised with carrots, celery, turnips, leeks, savoy cabbage and beans. During the hunting season, game dishes are offered, including venison, hare, and pigeon (*pigeonneaux à l'ardennaise*), pheasants cooked Brussels-style (larded, with vine leaves and bacon) and wild hare Brussels-style (with Madeira and parsley).

Other delicacies to be found on the menu are duck pâté with port, game pâté with wild mushrooms, quails with hop shoots, rabbit braised in Trappist beer or pigs' kidneys fried with juniper berries. There is also a large selection of Belgian cheeses: Remoudou made with double cream, Lo Abbey cheese, Santon, goat's cheese from Limburg, Mandjes cheese (made from skimmed milk), the strong-tasting Aette – or the mild *fromage au bureai*, a cheese made from buttermilk.

There is a wide choice of good wines at reasonable prices, and even house wines are frequently of high quality. Most of the wine which is drunk in Brussels comes from France. The desserts are excellent, and the meal is rounded off with coffee and delicious chocolates. When it comes to enjoying chocolates, as well as consuming champagne, the people of Brussels are world champions.

They are also very fond of sweets and snacks, and it is said that they consume 13 kg of pure chocolate per year each on average. Brussels' specialities include its famous *gaufres*, waffles eaten with sugar or syrup, which are particularly delicious when you buy them freshly prepared from stands in the streets. Also highly recommended are the toffee sweets, babeluttes, and of course shortbread of every shape, to suit every taste.

A brief look back into history reveals why this is such a culinary wonderland. Before the 16th century there was hardly any such thing as French cuisine, let alone Belgian. Sauces were strongly spiced, to disguise the pungent aroma of the meat. The wine accompanying meals was more reminiscent of vinegar than grape juice. The chief characteristic of the medieval cuisine indulged in by the rich was that it lay heavy in the stomach. Then along came the two Medici ladies, Catherine and Maria, as the wives of French kings, bringing their own cooks from Florence with them to the French court. The resultant culinary revolution spread to Ghent, Bruges, Antwerp and Brussels. Flemish cuisine combined with Italian in an almost exemplary way – and we are still enjoying the result. And once the sea route to India had been discovered, there was a constant supply of pepper, cinnamon, nutmeg and other exotic spices. The virtues of vegetables – formerly regarded as suitable only for women and the poor, and as being injurious to male health – were also discovered. Indigenous vegetables were now joined by imported broccoli, lemons, artichokes, green beans and tomatoes. As Victor Hugo, the author of *Les Misérables*, sat in a restaurant not far from the barricades, eating one piece of bread after another, he heard a neighbouring diner remark "Only a Frenchman could eat so much bread". Whereupon the writer, who was living in exile in Brussels, retorted: "Only someone from Brussels could eat so much of everything."

In most restaurants there are certain times of the day when it is difficult to find a free table if you arrive unannounced. So always make sure you reserve well in advance.

RESTAURANTS CATEGORY I

(A meal for one, of several courses without drinks, approximately Bfr 1,350)

L'Albon Chambon (107/E3)
In the traditional *Metropole* Hotel, genuine art deco style restaurant. Pleasant and very elegant. *Closed Sat–Sun, Place de Brouckère 31, Tel. 217 76 50, Metro: De Brouckère*

Auberge de Boendael (U/C5)
Furnished in simple, rustic style, this converted farmhouse serves excellent meals, including games

Chips, Belgium's national dish

They are as popular with King Albert as with his subjects, they make an excellent snack between meals, and even the best haute cuisine chefs do not consider themselves above serving these crisp, golden, sticks of potato as an accompaniment to wild pigeon. Whether you call them *chips, frites, patat, pommes frites, Fritten, French fries or frieten*, if well-cooked, there is nothing to beat them: they must be hot, crisp on the outside, with no after-taste or smell of oil. For best results they must be made from freshly sliced potatoes and fried in clean oil.

The classical recipe: peel potatoes and slice up into sticks. Fry in a deep fryer at 160°C for four minutes. Remove from oil and drain on kitchen paper, leave aside for 30 minutes. Then finish frying at 190°C until golden brown. Season to taste.

Gourmet Restaurants in Brussels

Bruneau (102/B4)
This restaurant is named after its three-star chef Jean-Pierre Bruneau, who cooks with style and confidence. Should you succeed in booking a table, go for the specialities of the day rather than the à la carte menu. From Bfr 3,250. *Closed Tue evening and Wed lunchtime. Avenue Broustin 73, Tel. 427 69 78, Metro: Simonis*

Comme chez Soi (107/D5)
To get a table at this restaurant, with Belgium's top chef is an experience in itself and, for once, paying the bill is a pleasure. Many of the dishes have flavours clearly inspired by the Far East. To eat a meal cooked by Pierre Wynant is a real treat. His restaurant, decorated in art nouveau style, has been a place of pilgrimage for gourmets for more than twenty years. Menu from Bfr 2,150. *Closed Sun and Mon, Place Rouppe 23, Tel. 512 29 21, Metro: Anneessens*

La Maison du Cygne (107/E4)
The most beautiful restaurant in the world in the most beautiful square in the world. The view from the first floor over the Grand' Place is a very special experience. The cuisine is classical French, and the daily recommendations are sure to please. There are good value menus at lunchtimes. Menu from Bfr 2,200. *Closed Sat lunchtime and Sun, Grand' Place 9, Tel. 511 82 44, Metro: Gare Centrale*

L'Écailler du Palais Royal (107/F5)
The finest and best fish restaurant in the city. Well travelled gourmets even insist that it is the best in the world. The art of cooking at L'Ecailler can best be described as creativity combined with know-how. The house speciality *Ravioli de homard au curry léger* is delicious. Excellent and imaginative dishes include Scottish salmon or sole *à l'écrasée*, and the shrimp croquettes are an absolute must. The first floor of the restaurant is purely classic, but some concessions are made to more popular tastes on the ground floor. A complete meal will cost you Bfr 3,200. *Closed Sun and public holidays, rue Bodenbroek 18, Tel. 512 87 51, tram: 92, 93, 94*

Sea Grill (107/F3)
This is especially popular for its fresh range of sea fish, lobsters and oysters. If all the tables are taken in this post-modern, somewhat imposing hotel restaurant, it can be cramped. Thanks to star chef Jacques Le Divellec the restaurant has won many awards, and has become very well known, and not only to Eurocrats and lobbyists. Its specialities include Breton lobster, and goose liver with braised shallots. From Bfr 1,750. *Closed Sat and Sun, in the Radisson SAS Hotel, rue Fossé-aux-Loups 47, Tel, 227 31 20, Metro: Gare Centrale*

specialities from the Ardennes. *Closed Sat and Sun, Square du Vieux Tilleul 12 (at the edge of the city), Tel. 672 70 55*

Les Baguettes Impériales (101/D4)
High quality Vietnamise cuisine. The art of cookery as practised by Madame Ma Huu Duy is so sophisticated that even the chauvinistic French have awarded this exotic restaurant one star. The secret of its refinement lies in the combination of Flemish and Vietnamese elements. *Closed Tue and Sun evening, Avenue J. Sobiesky 70, Tel. 479 67 32, Metro: Stuyvenbergh*

Barbizon (U/D5)
In an idyllic setting in the middle of the Brabant landscape, this restaurant is worth the journey if you want to get away from Brussels. Wild boar specialities according to season. Elegantly furnished. *Closed Tue and Wed, Welriekendedreef 95 (Forêt de Soignes), 3090 Jesus-Eik, Tel. 657 04 62, go by taxi/car*

Bonsoir Clara (107/D3)
★ This stylish bistro is quite trendy, quite good and quite expensive. Mediterranean cuisine presented with Belgian flair. *Open daily, rue Antoine Dansaert 22, Tel. 502 09 90, Metro: Bourse*

Brigitinnes (107/E5)
A *brasserie* in art deco style. Daily specials depending on what the market has to offer, good value for money. *Closed Sat and Sun lunchtimes, Place de la Chapelle 5, Tel. 512 68 91, Metro: Gare Centrale, bus 20*

At Pierre Wynant's gourmets feel quite at home

Castello Banfi **(107/F5)**
Serving Italian cuisine in art deco surroundings, this restaurant enjoys a good reputation. Why not try the spaghetti with caviar? *Closed Sun evening and Mon, rue Bodenbroek 12, Tel. 512 87 94, tram: 92, 93, 94*

Claude Dupont **(102/A4)**
★ An address steeped in tradition, an elegant mansion with upper class pretensions. The cooking is conservative, but it is not unheard of for curry and saffron to be used for flavouring. Even so, the culinary accent remains firmly on Belgian specialities. *Closed Mon and Tue, Avenue Vital Riethuisen 46 (near the Basilica), Tel. 426 00 00, tram: 19*

L'Idiot du Village **(107/E5)**
High standards of behaviour are expected here, although jeans are allowed. The Breton chef serves up some surprising combinations: hare with shrimps, pigeons with peas, and goose liver with mussels. The clientele is chic and successful. There is a good atmosphere and the service is an added attraction in itself. Reservation essential. *Closed Sat and Sun, rue Notre Seigneur 19, Tel. 502 55 82, Metro Anneessens*

La Manufacture **(107/D3)**
One of the city's trendiest establishments. The décor and the clientele exude chic. Cuisine à la mode: lamb and crayfish with curried fruits, salmon with yoghurt. Large wine selection – at a high price. As in all fine restaurants, French is spoken here. *Closed Sat lunchtime and Sun., rue Notre-Dame du Sommeil 12–22, Tel. 502 25 25,Metro: Ste-Catherine*

Meyers Michel **(U/D4)**
Chic bistro, everything here is thoroughly stylish, including the clientele. A must for lovers of seafood. Situated near the Parc de Tervuren. *Closed Sun, Avenue Orban 231, Tel. 770 41 30, go by taxi/car.*

Mon Manège à Toi **(U/D4)**
Whilst tasty food is of course a pre-requisite, restaurant owners still need something eccentric to attract attention. In this case merry-go-round horses help to create the *ambience*. The restaurant also has a garden. *Closed Sat and Sun, rue Neerveld 1, Tel. 770 02 38, Metro: Roodebeek*

Moulin de Lindekemale **(U/D4)**
This gourmet restaurant is furnished in rustic style, and is located in an old windmill on the edge of the city. Always full, always good. Lamb and game when in season. *Closed Sat and Sun, Avenue J.F. Debecker 6, Tel. 770 90 57, go by taxi/car*

L'Ogenblik **(107/E3)**
★ You would be hard put to, to find bistro cuisine as good as this in Paris: wide variety, new dishes daily, comfortable atmosphere, and popular for more than twenty years. Fish specialities dominate the menu in summer, game in the winter. Furnished with marble tables, the salt barrel is the only decorative feature. At lunchtime you can order excellent daily specials for about Bfr 550. *Closed Sun, Galerie des Princes 1, Tel. 511 61 51, Metro: De Brouckère*

Les 4 Saisons **(107/E4)**
It is not often that a hotel restau-

rant gains a name in its own right, but this one has – even if the décor leaves something to be desired. The restaurant is small and dark. Lunch from Bfr 1,890. *Closed Sat lunchtime and Sun, rue de l'Homme Chrétien 2 (Royal Windsor Hotel) Tel. 505 51 00, bus 95, 96, Metro: Gare Centrale*

Rugbyman No. 2 **(107/D3)**
Lobster, lobster and yet more lobster. A classic, expensive fish restaurant with the accent on oysters and lobster, served "flamed" "with whiskey" or "à la Flamande" at prices starting from Bfr 1,550. The restaurant seats 80, who have to be crammed in, and the service could be better. *Open daily, Quai aux Briques 12, Tel. 512 37 60, Metro: Ste-Catherine*

Sirène d'Or **(107/D3)**
A modern restaurant serving classical dishes cooked to a high standard. Bouillabaisse a speciality. *Closed Sun and Mon, Place Sainte-Catherine 1 A, Tel. 513 51 98, Metro: Ste-Catherine*

Taverne du Passage **(107/E3)**
This art deco brasserie is a Brussels institution. Families meet here for Sunday brunch, and visitors and EU officials alike enjoy the classic bourgeois cuisine. The waiters can be quite brusque and brash. *Open daily, Galerie de la Reine 30, Tel. 512 37 32, Metro: Gare Centrale*

Trente Rue de la Paille **(107/E5)**
This rustic, comfortable restaurant is where gourmets get together to enjoy tried and tested dishes. However: tradition has its price. *Closed Sat and Sun, rue de la Paille 30 (Sablon), Tel. 512 07 15, bus: 20*

RESTAURANTS CATEGORY 2

(Average cost of a meal without wine: Bfr 950)

L'Amadeus **(112/A3)**
This highly individual restaurant is housed in a former picture workshop. Its owner, the architect Neirynek, has combined every possible style. Under the chandeliers, the diners are mostly young and self-assured. The food is simple but imaginative, and includes mussels and oysters from Brittany. *Closed Mon, rue Veydt 13, Tel. 538 34 27, tram 92*

Au Chat Perché **(107/E4)**
Attractive establishment, serving simple lunches, such as crêpes, salads and quiches, at moderate prices. There are also vegetarian dishes on the menu. In the evening candlelight makes for a more romantic atmosphere, and if you are lucky, there may be a jazz band. *Open Tue–Fri midday–2.30 pm and 5 pm–11 pm, Sat 5–11 pm, closed mid-July–Aug, rue de la Samaritaine 20, Tel. 513 52 13, tram: 92, 93, 94*

Aux Armes de Bruxelles **(107/E3)**
★ One of Brussels' classic restaurants. Plush furnishings with plenty of oak, and diners who match the style. Brussels specialities such as *waterzooi* (fish stew); the steaks are prepared with beer. The restaurant is famous for its grilled turbot and mussels in wine sauce, *moules spéciales* with chips. The waiters here still wear white jackets with large, gold epaulettes. *Closed*

Mon, rue des Bouchers 13, Tel. 511 55 98, Metro: Bourse

Astrid Chez Pierrot **(108/B3)**
A comfortable, atmospheric bistro. Daniel and Pierre Brack, two ambitious chefs, provide meals at amazingly reasonable prices. *Closed Sun, rue de la Presse 21, Tel. 217 38 31, Metro: Madou*

La Belle Maraîchère **(107/D3)**
A restaurant with plenty of fish dishes to enjoy. The atmosphere is hectic, with the staff often working flat out, but you should not let that worry you. Speciality: fish soup. *Closed Mon and Tue, Place Ste-Catherine 11, Tel. 512 97 59, Metro: Ste-Catherine*

Café du Dôme **(107/F2)**
★ This well established restaurant with art nouveau elements is particularly popular with people in their late twenties and those who are watching their figure, as it serves low-calorie cuisine. Daily specials approximately Bfr 450. *Closed Sun. Boulevard Botanique 13, Tel. 218 45 29, Metro: Rogier*

Chez Henri **(107/D2)**
Popular fish restaurant. Monkfish with vegetables, casserole of mussels. *Open daily, rue de Flandre, Tel. 219 64 15, Metro: Ste-Catherine*

Chez Jacques **(107/D2)**
One of the last original fish bars in the fish market. Quite simple, quite small, with a happy atmosphere. The five variations on mussels taste good, so does the fresh salmon. Reservation essential! *Closed Sun, Quai aux Briques 44, Tel. 513 27 62, Metro: Ste-Catherine*

L'Etoile d'Or **(106/C4)**
★ This is one of the few remaining guesthouses in Brussels that still has a wooden floor and cast iron stove. It serves not only delicious, solid Belgian specialities, but also Spanish dishes – depending on the chef's mood. *Closed Sat and Sun lunchtime, rue des Foulons 30, Tel. 502 60 48, Metro: Anneessens*

Halloween **(107/E4)**
★ If you want a restaurant that will terrify you, or give you the creeps, look no further. In these gloomy rooms customers dine in the company of mythical creatures and the waiters, dressed as monks, address them as *frère* (brother) and *sœur* (sister). However the food is thoroughly enjoyable, examples being chicken with fresh-water crabs, smoked duck or chicken with artichokes. *Closed Sun, rue des Grands Carmes 10, Tel. 514 12 56, Metro: Anneessens.*

Kasbah **(107/D3)**
With its sensuous aromas and dark furnishings, this popular establishment entices diners in with its Moroccan specialities. Guests enjoy their food in a chic atmosphere seated at long tables, on two floors. *Closed Sat and Sun lunchtime, rue A. Dansaert 20, Tel. 502 40 26, Metro: Bourse*

Marmiton **(107/E3)**
Situated in the city's most popular district for restaurants, this establishment, furnished in warm colours, is one of only about half a dozen that are still also frequented by natives of Brussels. Its traditional dishes include grilled fish specialities which can be enjoyed on the

pavement in the city's most beautiful arcade. *Open daily, rue des Bouchers 43, Tel. 511 79 11, Metro: Gare Centrale*

Petits Oignons **(107/E5)**
An unpretentious restaurant, typical of the Marolles district which is thought by some to be in need of redevelopment. The service is friendly and the food good. *Closed Sun, rue Notre-Seigneur 13, Tel. 512 47 38, bus: 20*

La Quincaillerie **(112/A4)**
★ The expensive food here is upstaged by the pretty waitresses. This former ice products shop has become one of the most individualistic brasseries in the city. Large wine selection. The customers of this ultra-fashionable restaurant dress in casual but expensive clothes. Reservation is absolutely essential, and the bill tends to amount to more than you would expect. From Bfr 1,750. *Closed Sun lunchtime, full meal from Bfr 1,750, rue du Page 45, Tel. 538 25 53, bus: 60*

In t'Spinnekopke **(107/D3)**
A cheerful old city inn, serving Belgian dishes such as *lapin á la gueuze* ("rabbit in Gueuze beer") which is always delicious. *Closed Sun, Place du Jardin aux Fleurs 1, Tel. 511 86 95, Metro: Bourse*

Au Stekerlapatte **(111/E1)**
★ Tucked away in a dark street behind the massive *Palais de Justice* this cosy bistro is a trendy meeting place for writers, journalists, actors and artists. Customers sit cheek by jowl, there is a good atmosphere, and the food is tasty. Dishes include calf's kidneys, chicken cooked Brussels style, or other à la carte specialities, at prices starting from Bfr 950. *Closed Mon, rue des Prêtres, Tel. 512 86 81, Metro: Hôtel des Monnaies*

The variety of fish dishes is simply endless

Les Trois Chicons **(111/D1)**
A comfortable, popular restaurant in the heart of the Marolles district. Its specialities are dishes with endives *(chicon)*, the Flemish national vegetable. A must to try: pheasant with braised endives. *Closed Mon, rue des Renards 9–11, Tel. 511 55 83, Metro: Porte de Hal*

Ultième Hallucinatie **(104/B6)**
★ This bistro is furnished entirely in art nouveau style. You can meet over a beer or coffee, or in the restaurant. Late in the evening the bistro is often full to bursting. Specialities include *turbot à la gueuze* and duck breast with black peppercorns. The restaurant's *ambience* is reflected in the prices. *Closed Sat lunchtime and Sun, rue Royale 316, Tel. 217 06 14, tram: 92, 93, 94*

A Champagne among Beers

You cannot simply walk into a pub in Brussels and order "a beer". You have to say whether you want, for example, a Kwak, a Gueuze, a Lambic or a Trappist. The beer lists in the "staminekes" or "estaminets" have a large number of speciality beers. These are beers that are savoured slowly, with appreciation, and not simply downed one glass after another. You can order a beer in the finest of restaurants without causing eyebrows to be raised, and at festive receptions it is regarded as good form to serve beer as well as juices, wine or champagne. No one, including the king and the prime minister, is above raising a glass in public to toast "Prince Gambrinus", the patron of beer drinkers.

It is estimated that there are about 300 speciality beers, produced by 123 breweries, with more than 160 flavours, roughly divided into Weissbeer, Alt, Trappist, monastery beer, Faro, Lambic, Tripel, Kriek, Ale, Gueuze, Stout, Scotch or Pilsener. Pilsener is here regarded as an "everyday" beer. Brussels certainly deserves its unofficial title of "Beer Capital".

Le Vistro **(107/D2)**
Pleasant fish restaurant. The day's specials are written on a blackboard, and customers eat at bistro tables. Lunch from Bfr 250. *Closed Sat lunchtime and Sun, Quai aux Briques 16, Tel. 512 41 81, Metro: Ste-Catherine*

RESTAURANTS CATEGORY 3

(Average cost of a meal without wine: Bfr 600)

Au Brueghel **(111/D2)**
Brussels tavern, facing the ancient city gate, Porte de Hal. Very popular with the local residents, it serves mussels with chips and the dish of the day for about Bfr 495. A simple but busy place, where people go to chat over a beer or coffee. *Open daily, Boulevard du Midi 145, Tel. 534 59 76, Metro: Porte de Hal.*

Faste Fou **(111/E1)**
A modern bistro, very trendy and chic. Little snacks and exquistic salads. *Closed Sun, rue du Grand-Cerf 21, Tel 511 38 32, Metro: Louise*

La Grande Ecluse **(107/C5)**
Trendy restaurant in the engine room of a former sluice (open to the public). Also serves vegetarian meals, wonderful desserts and expensive wine. The cuisine is good, and the portions generous. *Closed Sat lunchtime and Sun, Boulevard Poincaré 77, Tel. 522 30 25, Metro: Zuid*

t' Kelderke **(107/E4)**
In the cellar of this historical 16th century building on the Grand' Place things really liven up in the evenings. Specialities include Belgian dishes such as *waterzooi* or *carbonnade à la flamande* ("beef in beer"). *Open daily, Grand' Place 15, Tel. 513 73 44*

Oyster Bar **(107/F1)**
An elegant snack bar serving nothing but a wide selection of oysters fresh from the sea. Occasionally it also has home-made *foie gras.* Popular at lunchtimes. *Closed Sun, Passage du Nord (on the rue Neuve), Metro: De Brouckère*

Le Paon **(107/E4)**
A restaurant with a good atmosphere, offering good quality food. Seats about 109. If you like, you can book for a Bruegel evening – with plenty of meat, beer, music and traditional costumes as seen in Bruegel's paintings. *Open daily, Grand' Place 35, Tel. 513 35 82, Metro: Bourse*

PP Café **(107/D-E3)**
Like the *Archiduc* piano bar or the *La Cigogne* bistro, this is one of the many fashionable establishments in the lower city between the stock exchange and the fish market. Hearty one-course meals and salad platters for about Bfr 350. A passageway leads through to the Kladaradatsch Palace, a tavern with a cinema, a trendy meeting place which is something quite special. *Open daily, rue J. van Praet 26, Tel. 514 25 62, Metro: Bourse*

Tapas Locas **(106/E4)**
Spanish tapas bar with an impressive selection of delicious snacks at moderate prices. *Open daily, rue du Marché au Charbon 74, Tel. 502 12 68. Metro: De Brouckère, Bourse*

Totem **(106/D4)**
Small vegetarian restaurant with delicious soups, cakes and wines at reasonable prices. *Open Wed–Sun 2 pm–11 pm, rue des Grands Charme 6, Tel. 513 11 52, Metro: Bourse*

Natives of Brussels enjoy relaxing outside the pavement cafés

Shopping with style

Brussels' shopping centre is world class, with historical arcades, chic boulevards, flea markets and antiques

Going shopping in Brussels is something of an experience. Apart from the numerous weekly markets and shopping arcades, it is primarily the countless small and above all original shops that make it what it is. Commercial life, like everything else about Brussels, has its own particular character. There is certainly no shortage of money in this expanding city. This is brought home to outsiders by the extravagant shops and the high prices. There is a huge contrast between different quality levels: shops where goods can be purchased at reasonable prices, and some which are sinfully expensive and completely over the top. Magnificent, glittering jewellers' shops, ultramodern fashion boutiques with the most up to date models, thoroughly stylish antique shops with treasures from the past. The districts around St. Gery and the Marolles in the lower city, which were somewhat run down have now developed into shopping centres to suit unusual and expensive tastes.

The main shopping areas take in *Boulevard Waterloo, Avenue Louise,* and *Place Stéphanie* in the upper city, and *Boulevard Max, rue Neuve, rue A. Dansaert, Place De Brouckère* in the lower city. The two centres are connected by numerous small streets such as *rue de Namur,* and *Marché-aux-Herbes.* There are also indoor shopping centres, known here as galleries, with good retail shops, and well supplied with bistros and cafés. The most beautiful and the oldest are the *Galeries St-Hubert* near the Grand' Place, which is divided up into the *Galerie des Princes, Galerie du Roi* and *Galerie de la Reine.* In contrast new indoor shopping centres are to be found at the *Centre Anspach,* the *Centre Monnaie,* the *rue Neuve* and, in the upper city as you come from the Louise Metro station: *Galerie de la Porte Louise, Galerie d'Ixelles* and *Galerie de la Toison d'Or.*

The antiques district spreads out from around the *Place du Grand Sablon* with its small side streets.

Hours are flexible, with most shops being open *Monday to Saturday from 10 am–6 or 6.30 pm; on Fridays some supermarkets do not close until 8 or 9 pm.* Some shops also open on Sundays: for example bakeries, small grocers' shops, and also supermarkets from 9 am to 1 pm. Payment is made in Belgian francs (Bfr), with

Every conceivable luxury under one roof: the Galeries Saint-Hubert

Eurocheques (never a problem) or credit cards, if expressly indicated in the shop.

ANTIQUARIAN BOOKSHOPS

Artemys **(107/E4)**
A bookshop especially for women with feminist literature from France, the Netherlands, America and Germany. *Galerie Bortier 8–10 (rue Saint-Jean), Metro: Bourse, Gare Centrale*

Bookmarket **(107/E4)**
Plenty of old books, including works in English can be found here. Specialist areas include art, cooking and crime, as well as computers. Very cramped and confusing to visitors, but the owners know their way around. Books can also be exchanged here. *Rue de la Madeleine 47, Metro: Gare Centrale*

FNAC **(107/F2)**
Large book store with a wide variety of literature, volumes on travel and art as well as comics – all in Dutch, French and German. *Rue Neuve City 2, Metro: Rogier*

Librairie Quatre Vents **(112/B6)**
This bookshop specialises in anything to do with horses and riding. *Avenue Legrand 80, tram: 23, 90, 93, 94*

Librairie van de Plas **(107/E4)**
The kind of second-hand bookshop you see in old engravings: dusty, mysterious and full of nooks and crannies. Enthusiasts in search of literature, art, old postcards or copper engravings will find it difficult to tear themselves away. *Rue des Éperonniers 10, Metro: Gare Centrale*

Papyrus **(107/E4)**
Book lovers will receive helpful advice in this bookshop which specialises in historical literature. *Galerie Bortier 16, Metro: Gare Centrale*

Posada **(107/E4)**
★ Huge selection of volumes on art and exhibition catalogues. An abundance of precious books on the theme of painting, old and modern art and architecture. The books are clearly arranged into categories. *Rue de la Madeleine 29, Metro: Bourse, Gare Centrale*

Tropismes **(107/E3)**
One of the best bookshops in the whole country; French literature piled high under golden ceilings. The staff are helpful and friendly. Also open on Sundays. *Galerie des Princes 11 (Galerie St-Hubert), Metro: Gare Centrale.*

ANTIQUES

Les Arts Décoratifs **(107/F5)**
This is where you will discover rare art deco objects, from cupboards, tables and lamps to ashtrays and coffee spoons. *Rue Lebeau 49, tram: 92, 93, 94*

Atmosphéres **(107/F5)**
Portraits and hunting trophies, Indian lamps, French and English 19th century furniture, souvenirs from the colonial era, all bargains at about Bfr 1,500. *Rue de Rollebeek 17, bus: 20 (Grand Sablon)*

Collectors Gallery **(107/F5)**
Everything conceivable in the

MARCO POLO SELECTION: SHOPPING

1 **Bernard**
A magnificent shop to delight any gourmet (page 61)

2 **Dandoy**
The aroma of Christmas baking pervades this shop every day (page 60)

3 **La Boutique de Tintin**
For the lover of comics this shop is a special treat (page 61)

4 **Francis Janssens – Van der Maelen**
An amazing variety of gleaming silverware (page 62)

5 **Rosalie Pompon**
An absolute paradise for lovers of miniatures (page 61)

6 **Place du Grand Sablon**
Plenty of antiques dear to the collector (page 64)

7 **Place du Jeu de Balle**
A lively, colourful flea market with bargains if you are lucky (page 64)

8 **Posada**
The widest possible collection of art books (page 58)

9 **Le Pain Quotidien**
A quite exceptional baker's shop (page 60)

10 **Vivace Piu**
The most colourful fashion house in Brussels (page 64)

way of toys made from sheet metal, tin soldiers and mechanical toys. *Rue Lebeau 19, tram: 92, 93, 94*

Costermans (107/F5)
Founded in 1839 and specializing in 18th century furniture, clocks and objets d'art. *Place du Grand Sablon, tram: 92, 93, 94*

Au fil du temps (107/F5)
Specialising in recorded works, Austrian furniture dating from 1900 and 19th c. ornaments. *Rue Lebeau 41, bus: 20 (Grand Sablon)*

Village des Antiquaires (107/F5)
About a dozen antique dealers here under one roof. The items on sale range from old toys, dolls, books, weapons, furniture and paintings. Jewellery is also on offer, but not always at fair prices. *Rue Bodenbroek 22 (near Grand Sablon), tram: 92, 93, 94*

BAKERS' SHOPS/PATISSERIES

The bakers' shops, which always smell wonderfully appetising, sell all kinds of delicacies and specialities. Boxes and packages of all shapes and sizes are piled high with Greek pastries, almond bread, "sand biscuits" with and without cinnamon, croissants, little rolls and cakes. And of course, *speculaas*, the spiced biscuits especially associated with Christmas, but available throughout the year. These specialities of Brussels make a tasty souvenir that will keep quite well.

Dandoy **(107/E3)**
★ 🚸 An enticing window display has child-sized *speculaas* figures, beautifully wrapped in cellophane. Inside, the narrow shop is piled high with all kinds of delicacies, which help to perpetuate the reputation of the Dandoys *speculaas* dynasty. *Petite Rue au Beurre 31, Metro: Bourse (branch establishment: rue Ch. Buls 14, Grand' Place)*

Le Pain Quotidien **(107/D3)**
★ A substantial breakfast can be eaten here from 7.30 am onwards. This is a chic bakery, in which a simple sandwich becomes a hedonistic treat, to be eaten for lunch or as a snack between meals. Open until 7.30 am. You can also buy rye bread and jam to take away. *Rue Antoine Dansaert 16, Metro: Bourse.* There are about a dozen branches, some of which can be found at the following addresses: *"Sablon", rue des Sablons 11, "Loi", rue de la Croix de Fer 53, or "Louise", Avenue Louise 124*

Tea for Two **(111/E4)**
Two intimate English tea-shops, where tea is served with cheesecake and other cakes and pastries. *Waterloose Steenweg 394, tram 91, 92 (Ma. Campagne)*

BRUSSELS LACE

A large selection of Brussels lace can be found in several shops on the Grand' Place. However, look closely at any special offers!

Ma. Belge de Dentelle **(107/E3)**
This shop has the most beautiful lace selection in Brussels. *Galerie de la Reine 6–8. Metro: Gare Centrale*

A nimble-fingered lace maker works at this old craft

Rosaline **(107/E3)**
Large selection of Brussels lace. *Marché-aux-Herbes 64, Metro: Gare Centrale*

COMICS

Brüsel **(107/E3)**
This shop is small, but has a large collection of recent French comics. *Boulevard Anspach 100, Metro: Bourse*

Multi B.D. **(107/D4)**
A shop stuffed full of booklets, books and souvenirs on the theme of comics, a genre that enjoys huge respect here. B.D. stands for *Bandes Dessinées*, as comic strips are called in French. Here you can find, in French, not only Tintin, Quick and Flupke, but also Asterix, Batman and Lucky Luke. *Boulevard Anspach 126–128, Metro: Bourse*

Sans Titre **(107/D5)**
Almost complete selection of comics and books for young

people. Artists' exhibitions. *Avenue de Stalingrad 8, Metro: Anneessens*

Slumberland **(107/F2)**
Bookshop in the Comic Museum. Everything imaginable to do with comic strip characters, such as T-shirts, figures and everything else for the comic enthusiast. *Closed Mon, rue des Sables 20, Metro: Gare Centrale, Botanique*

DELICATESSEN

L'Arbre à Vins **(O)**
This house has a tradition going back to 1805. It always has about 7,000 bottles of wine from the most famous wine-growing areas in stock. *Kolonel Chaltin 103, go by taxi/car*

Bernard **(108/A5)**
★ Lovers of truffles, Russian and Persian caviar, live lobsters, oysters and other delicacies from all over the world (all of whom are more numerous than you might think), come here to do their shopping. *Rue de Namur 93, Metro: Porte de Namur*

Bière Artisanale **(108/B6)**
If you are a keen beer drinker or if you are looking for a typical souvenir, this shop has a selection of 400 types of beer, each with its own special glass. *Chaussée de Wavre 174, Metro: Porte de Namur*

Le Petit Normand **(107/E3)**
Two of the finest delicatessens in Brussels face each other across the street. No. 8 sells cheese, and No. 5 delicious pâtés, Ardennes ham and succulent sausages. *Rue de Tabora 5 et 8, Metro: De Brouckère*

GIFTS & SOUVENIRS

La Boutique de Tintin **(107/E4)**
★ This gift shop is named after Belgium's most famous cartoon character, Tintin. Absolutely anything that is connected with Tintin, however tenuously, can be bought here, including T-shirts, figures, and comics in French. *Rue de la Colline 13, Metro: Gare Centrale*

Eurotempo **(107/E3)**
This shop sells absolutely anything connected in any way with a united Europe – printed and painted in the yellow and blue European colours: from egg cups to car stickers to the European umbrella. *Rue du Marché aux Herbes 52, Metro: Gare Centrale*

L'Objet du Désir **(107/E3)**
Miniature grandfather clocks, strange cut-throat razors, adhesive tape holders (Bfr 2,600), imitations of articles from the 1950s and other original items from futuristic design studios. *Rue de Tabora 14–16, Metro: De Brouckère*

Rosalie Pompon **(107/F5)**
★ Miniature works of art by well-known artists. A paradise for art lovers. *Rue Lebeau 65, tram: 92, 93*

Serneels **(111/F2)**
Toys are sold here, also for big children. Miniature zoos and over-sized zoos. Tintin bookends from Bfr 2,000. *Avenue Louise 69, Metro: Louise, tram 94*

Au Siffleur **(107/D5)**
This is where you will find things you never dreamt of. Unusual

goods, to say the least. *Rue des Tanneurs 141, bus: 20, 48*

GLASS & CROCKERY

Art et Sélection **(107/E3)**
The window display dazzles with the craziest items made from glass. The sweet boxes look just like fantastic chocolates. *Marché-aus-Herbes 83, Metro: Gare Centrale*

Francis Janssens – Van der Maelen **(107/F6)**
★ Old and new silverware can be found here, in overwhelming variety. You can even buy rare individual pieces from the *belle époque. Boulevard de Waterloo 26, Metro: Porte de Namur*

Jadoul **(112/A1)**
A large display shows all the expensive items needed to give style to the breakfast table. Well-known makes such as Christofle, Wedgwood, and Villeroy & Boch are represented here. Silver corkscrews are a snip from Bfr 5,000 upwards. *Avenue Louise 17, Metro: Louise*

INTERIOR ARCHITECTURAL DESIGN

A la Tentation **(107/E3)**
Fabrics and curtains, with floral designs predominating. *Galerie du Roi 29, Metro: Gare Centrale*

Dille & Kamille **(111/E2)**
Flowers, herbs, kitchen utensils made from steel, iron or wood – and in every style imaginable. *Rue Jean Stas 16, Metro: Louise*

Dujardin **(112/A2)**
Upholstery materials, fabrics for table cloths, and curtain materials. All the major international makes are represented. *Avenue Louise 82–84, Metro: Louise*

Ligne **(107/E3)**
Design furniture in clean-cut, simple style. Every piece a work of art, with prices to match. *Galerie de la Reine 12–16, Metro: Gare Centrale*

Linen House **(107/F5)**
Table cloths, towels or handkerchiefs made from coarse or fine linen. *Rue Bodenbroek 10, bus: 48 (Grote Zavel)*

New De Wolf **(111/D1)**
2,500 sq m supermarket for home furnishings. Pieces from England, Tuscany, Provence and elsewhere. *Rue Haute, bus 20, 48 (Kapelle)*

Noir d'Ivoire **(107/E4)**
Red, yellow and green mark the three floors of this extravagant furniture store, whose wares include Moroccan mosaics, and wrought iron chairs. *Rue Gasthuis 25–27, bus: 48 (St. Jan)*

ART GALLERIES

In recent years the capital of Brussels has developed into a lively trading centre for the arts. The quality of the exhibits varies considerably, and the prices are generally high. *Information on previews can be obtained from Art Diary, Rue de la Vanne 39, Tel. 524 11 94.*

Albert Baronian **(106/C3)**
This gallery sets the tone for the avant-garde. *Boulevard Barthélemy 20, Tel. 512 92 95, Metro: Bourse, tram: 18*

Brussels offers exclusiveness

Contrast **(107/E5)**
Representational and traditional, works by Souvraz, Alexander Detmar and Christoforou. *Open Mon–Sat midday–6 pm, rue Ernest Allard, Tel. 512 98 59, tram: 92, 93, 94*

Coppens & Van de Velde **(107/D3)**
Here the emphasis is on the tried and tested. Works by Keith Haring, Lichtenstein, Sam Francis, Panemarenko and Warhol. *Open Wed–Fri 2 pm–7 pm, Sat 11 am–6 pm, rue van Artevelde 41, Tel. 513 81 74, Metro: Bourse*

Fondation pour l'Architecture **(112/B3)**
Photos, mock-ups and representations of architecture housed in a former power station. *Open Tue–Fri 12.30 pm–7 pm, Sat and Sun 1 pm–7 pm, rue de l'Ermitage 55, Tel. 649 02 59, tram: 81, 82, 93, 94*

Galerie Catherine Mayeur **(111/D1)**
The most consistently avant-garde, with artists like Aldo Palazzolo, Henri Bassmadjian, Gilbert Fastnaekens. *Open Tue–Sat midday–6 pm, rue des Renards 15A, Tel. 513 06 29, Metro: Porte de Hal*

Galerie des Beaux-Arts **(107/F4)**
This gallery is run by the daughter of the famous artist Marcel Broodthaers. Artists such as Ensor, De Chirico. *Open Tue–Sat 11 am–6.30 pm, rue Ravenstein 20–22, Tel. 513 67 77, Metro: Gare Centrale*

Halles St-Géry **(107/D3)**
In 1881, when people still believed in the Iron Age, these halls were built of brick and cast iron. Restored and modernised, the building hosts cultural, musical and sporting events. A number of galleries, a bar, large TV screens and boutiques. *Irregular opening times, Place Saint-Géry, Metro: Bourse*

Kanal 20 **(106/C3)**
Six galleries in one building showing works by young Belgian and foreign artists. *Open Wed–Sat 2 pm–6 pm, Boulevard Bathélemy 20, Metro: Comte de Flandre*

LEATHER GOODS

Delvaux **(107/E3)**
Most famous name for leather goods which are beautifully made from select materials: elegant luggage, chic belts and elegant shoes. *Galerie de la Reine 31, Metro: Gare Centrale*

Ganterie Italienne **(107/E3)**
This is worth a visit just to see the shop, which dates back to 1890; exclusive leather gloves, *Galerie de la Reine 3, Metro: Gare Centrale*

MARKETS

Brussels' colourful and exotic variety as a shopping centre is also reflected in its numerous markets. If you include the weekly markets, the antique markets, the fruit, flower and flea markets in the suburbs, it has a surprisingly large number, about a hundred, all of them well supported. The most important, colourful and impressive from the visitor's point of view are the *Sunday morning bird market on the Grand' Place*, the *daily flea market on the Place du Jeu de Balle (Vossenplein)*, the *antiques market at weekends on the Grand Sablon* and the *Sunday market at the Gare du Midi*, with its exotic atmosphere.

Antiques, curiosities, toys and bric-à-brac
★ *Place du Jeu de Balle (Vossenplein)* (**107/D6**) *in the Marolles district, 7 am–2 pm.* ★ *Place du Grand Sablon* (**107/E5**), *Sat 9 am–6 pm, Sun 9 am–2 pm. Place Bara* (toys), *Sun 6 am–1 pm. Place Reine Astrid, Jette, Sun 6 am–1 pm* (toys)

Flowers, fruit and vegetables
Place Sainte-Catherine (**107/D3**), *daily 7 am–5 pm, Gare du Midi* (**106/B–C5**), *Sun 6 am–1 pm*

Paintings, jewellery and graphic arts
Rue d'Aumale, Anderlecht (**U/A–B4**), *Fri 7 am–1 pm. Place du Souverain, Auderghem, Thu 8 am–1 pm. Place Saint-Denis, Forest, Sat 9 am–1 pm. Place Dumont, Woluwe St-Lambert, Tue 7 am–12.30 pm*

Bird market
Grand' Place (**107/E3**), *Sun 7 am–2 pm. Place Saint-Denis* (**U/B5**), *Forest, Sat 9 am–1 pm*

Weekly market in Woluwe St-Pierre (U/D4–5)
Foreigners come here to shop for delicious home-made pies, handmade cheeses, bread, or fish. *Tue, Fri and Sat 8 am–1 pm, Dumonplein in Woluwe, to the east of Brussels*

FASHION

Elvis Pompilio (107/E4)
Eccentric hat designer. This is where you will find classic, bold and funny hats. *Rue du Lombard 18, Metro: Bourse, bus 48*

Kwasi (107/D3)
Unusual and brightly coloured clothes and shoes for men. *Place Saint-Géry 18, Metro: Bourse*

Nathalie Vincent (107/D3)
Ladies' fashions which have a masculine touch. *Rue A. Dansaert 84, Metro: Bourse*

Planet One (107/F6)
Unusual and affordable clothes for discos and clubs. *Avenue de la Toison d'Or, Metro: Porte de Namur*

Privé Joke (107/D4)
Gear for young people, with a background cacophany of "techno" music. *Rue des Riches Claires 8, Metro: Bourse*

Stijl Men & Women (107/D3)
Flemish Haute Couture, with wit and style, unique in Brussels. *Rue Antoine Dansaert 74, Metro: Bourse*

Vivace Piu (112/A2)
★ The most colourful fashion house in the whole city. The unusual collection ranges from canary yellow, through grass green and sky blue to fiery red.

The clothes are simply tailored, most being made from linen. *Avenue Louise 43, Metro: Louise*

MUSIC

The Collector Record Movie **(107/E3)**
Rarities include old hits as well as a large selection of film music. Also hand-picked second-hand goods. Pre-war records on sale from Bfr 100. *Rue de la Bourse 26, Metro: Bourse*

DiscoSold **(107/F2)**
Second-hand records and CDs. *Boulevard Adophe-Max 67, Metro: Rogier*

Music-Way **(107/E3)**
The latest, the newest and the best on CD. *Also open Sun from 1.30 pm. Galerie du Roi 14, Metro: Gare Centrale*

CHOCOLATES & SWEETS

Scarcely anyone visiting Brussels will leave without taking with them some of its famous chocolates, whose main ingredients are cream and, of course, chocolate. These tasty souvenirs can be bought at almost every street corner. The quality is high and they are available in a wide variety of different flavours.

Godiva **(107/E3)**
A classic establishment which has raised chocolate production to an art form. The range on offer comprises ninety different varieties. An expensive brand with a good image. There are five branches in Brussels, one of them at *Grand' Place 22, Metro: Gare Centrale*

Leonidas **(107/E3)**
Leonidas' creamy and rather sweet tasting chocolates are regarded as part of the nation's staple diet. About 6,000 tonnes of chocolate are processed by the largest confectioner of all, to produce the chocolates which are marketed in 25 variations. Branches all over the city, two of them at *Boulevard Anspach* and *Adophe-Max, Metro: De Brouckère*

Mary **(107/F4)**
With its elegant blue and gold décor, sophisticated and expensive sweets, this is the finest of all sweet shops. *Closed Mon, Rue Royale 73, bus: 63*

Neuhaus **(107/E3)**
Amongst chocolate manufacturers, this establishment has a long tradition. An aristocratic brand with an annual turnover of several millions, and one of its branches can be found in the *Galeries St-Hubert, Metro: Gare Centrale*

Pierre Marcolini **(107/E5)**
The most daring flavours, including not only cocoa and tea, but even thyme and lavendar. Exclusive chocolate *haute cuisine. Place du Grand Sablon 39, tram: 92, 93, 94*

Planète Chocolat **(107/E4)**
A wide variety of hand-crafted chocolates with a high cocoa content. *Closed Mon, rue du Lombard 24, Metro: Bourse*

Wittamer **(107/E5)**
An overwhelming range of chocolates, cakes, and petits fours. A speciality of this master baker is the excellent chocolate cake from Bfr 600. *Place du Grand Sablon 12, tram: 92, 93, 94*

HOTEL AMIGO
Hôtel Amigo

A good night's sleep

Whether art deco or modern, the range is enormous, but even with over 130 hotels, this is still not enough

The hotels of Brussels reflect the cosmopolitan life of the city. More conventions are held in Brussels, seat of the EU and NATO, than in any other city apart from London and Paris. It is also Belgium's most important tourist centre. This is apparent from the city's range of hotels, which is truly international. Brussels has them all: the anonymous hotel chain Ramada, the fine artist's guesthouse Art Siru, the super-modern Radisson SAS, or the classical *belle époque* building exemplified by the Astoria. At present there are about 20,000 beds. But this is still not enough to meet the demand, and so new hotels are always being built, and old houses restored, such as the ornate neo-rococo style Le Plaza in the city centre.

Room prices in Brussels are comparable with those in Amsterdam, Rome or London. During the week it is absolutely essential to book in advance.

Popular with diplomats: the luxurious, plush hotel Amigo on the Grand' Place

Apart from price, location is often an important factor, for tourists and business people alike. It is therefore important to decide whereabouts in the city you want to stay, and then to find the right hotel in that district. The most popular area is around the Grand' Place or the upper city. However a hotel just outside Brussels can also be attractive. Many still retain their original décor, although the rooms are equipped with every modern convenience. And now that tradition and nostalgia have again become marketable commodities, modern businesses are slowly catching on. Discreet luxury, which is one of Brussels' strengths, is even being used by the anonymous "accommodation factories" which are run by computer, in competition with each other. An example of this can be found in the centre by the station, where modern developers are constructing an historical façade, with contemporary hotel rooms behind: small and practical, but above all efficient. Brussels hotels have far more double rooms than single. Single rooms are often tiny and badly laid out. In the last few years the rooms of most hotels have been renovated, as guests have become more demanding and tourism has become an increasingly important source of income. Weekends in Brussels are also by no means boring, there is always lots to do – the museums are open and there are plenty of street markets – and so it is well worth investigating special weekend offers. Most hotel groups offer bargain breaks when the rooms usually cost only one third or half the prices listed. Except in the case of a few large hotels, the room price also includes an extensive breakfast/buffet. The breakfast is usually good, the hotels generally have a bar, restaurant or bistro and even air conditioning. The staff are usually multilingual, friendly and helpful. Credit cards are accepted just about everywhere. The extensive hotel infrastructure also means that there is plenty for young people to do. Free hotel booking: *B.T.R., B.P. 41, B-1000 Brussels 23, Tel. 0032/2/513 74 84, Fax 513 92 77.* Prices indicated are for a double room with breakfast.

HOTELS CATEGORY 1

(for those who expect a high standard, double room Bfr 8,000–15,5000)

Amigo **(107/E4)**
★ This large, 178-room traditional hotel, which was formerly characterised by the

MARCO POLO SELECTION: HOTELS

1 **Amigo**
Traditional, luxury hotel very popular with diplomats (page 68)

2 **Château du Lac**
Fairy tale castle situated in quiet countryside (page 69)

3 **Dôme I & II**
Lively, modern house with style and flair (page 72)

4 **Manos**
Flair and *ambience* built around an intimate garden (page 72)

5 **Le Dixseptième**
This former residence of the Spanish ambassador has been turned into the most delightful hotel (page 69)

6 **Président Centre**
In a good location, with friendly staff, this is the best in its category (page 72)

7 **Les Bluets**
Family hotel with plenty of character. Pretty pink décor (page 72)

8 **Vendôme**
A mansion renowned for its own individual style (page 74)

9 **Welcome**
A small house with a lovely atmosphere and good food (page 74)

10 **Metropole**
Palatial hotel dating from the *belle époque*. Very good value at weekends (page 69)

gloomy atmosphere of the Spanish Renaissance, has been refurbished and generally brightened up. The foyer is still dreadfully plush, but the rooms are spacious and furnished in Empire style. In spite of its size the hotels is very charming. It has an underground car park and the weekend prices merit investigation. Its location on the Grand' Place is unbeatable. *Rue de l'Amigo 1–3, Tel. 547 47 47, Fax 513 52 77, Metro: Bourse*

Astoria (108/B3)
A palatial hotel in the style of the *belle époque.* The rooms are spacious and the restaurant *Le Palais Royal,* is enchanting with its nostalgic splendour. 118 rooms and royal suite with a black bath. From Bfr 12,000. *Rue Royale 103, Tel. 227 05 05, Fax 217 11 50, Metro: Botanique, Gare Centrale*

Bedford (107/D4)
Renovated and inviting: a centrally situated city hotel, modern, and catering for tourists and business people alike. *302 rooms, rue du Midi 135, Tel. 512 78 40, Fax 514 17 59, Metro: Bourse*

Bristol Stephanie (112/A2)
This hotel is centrally situated among the finest shopping streets, which also means that it is quieter in the evenings. The 142 rooms, which are not too small, are bright and modern. The service is very obliging. *Avenue Louise 91–93, Tel. 543 33 11, Fax 538 03 07, tram: 93, 94, Metro: Louise*

Château du Lac (U/D6)
★ This magnificent small castle in the fairy tale style of the turn of the 19th/20th century is situated about 20 minutes' drive from the city centre. This is the right place if you want to combine art, sport and culinary enjoyment, as the hotel has facilities for golf and tennis, and in addition an elegant restaurant *Le Trèfle à 4. 121 rooms, Avenue du Lac 87, 1332 Genval, Tel. 655 71 11, Fax 655 74 44*

Le Dixseptième (107/E4)
★ Situated almost directly on the Grand' Place. This was the former residence of the Spanish ambassador. It has a staircase in Louis XVI style, elegant drawing rooms, and rooms furnished with modern facilities as well as some antiques. Chic and elegant. Delicious breakfast. Special weekend offers! *24 rooms, rue de la Madeleine 25, Tel. 502 57 44, Fax 502 64 24, Metro: Gare Centrale*

Jolly Hotel du Grand Sablon (107/E4)
This 201 room hotel is the most spectacular to have been built during the last few years. Centrally situated, in the immediate vicinity of the Museum of Traditional and Modern Art. *Rue Bodenbroek 2–4, Tel. 512 88 00, Fax 512 67 66, tram: 92, 93, 94*

Metropole (107/E3)
★ Dating back to 1895, this is the oldest hotel in Brussels, and is situated in the centre. This famous building, which has now been restored, positively glows with *belle époque* splendour. The guests are no less distinguished, as a glance at the visitors' book will confirm: Sarah Bernhardt, Arthur Rubinstein and Charles De Gaulle have all checked in

here. The spirit of the *belle époque* in the foyer and *Alban Chambon* restaurant, is unfortunately missing from quite a number of the 410 rooms. *July–Aug special prices. Place De Brouckère 31, Tel. 217 23 00, Fax 218 02 20, Metro: De Brouckère*

Park Hotel **(109/F5)**
One of Brussels' few smaller family hotels. The house also

Luxury Hotels in Brussels

Conrad Brussels **(112/A2)**
In the chic upper city, the Conrad is regarded as the number one hotel on the square. This luxurious modern hotel is well but functionally furnished – and is ideal for EU diplomats and lobbyists to stay in on arrival. 269 rooms. From Bfr 13,000. *Avenue Louise 71, Tel. 542 42 42, Fax 542 42 00, Metro: Louise*

Hilton **(108/A6)**
Although it does belong to the famous hotel chain, this particular Hilton is in a class of its own. The rooms are large, furnished in contemporary style and have beautiful panoramic views over the city. The hotel has everything that the businessman or EU lobbyist could possibly need, including guaranteed anonymity. There are discounts for weekend stays. 430 rooms, from Bfr 8,700. *Boulevard de Waterloo 38, Tel. 504 11 11, Fax 504 21 11, Metro: Louise*

Meridien **(107/F4)**
Luxury class hotel at the station, with double glazing keeping out the street noise. Spacious rooms, excellent breakfast. Special weekend prices. 224 rooms. From Bfr 9,500. *Carrefour de l'Europe 3, Tel. 548 42 11, Fax 548 40 80, Metro: Gare Centrale*

Radisson SAS **(107/F3)**
A city hotel with modern facilities in a central, but quiet, location only a few steps away from the opera and the *Galeries Saint-Hubert*. The rooms are functional, but you can choose between Scandinavian, Asian, Italian or art deco furnishings. 281 rooms. From Bfr 12,000. *Rue du Fossé-aux-Loups 47, Tel. 219 28 28, Fax 219 62 62, Metro: De Brouckère*

Stanhope **(108/B5)**
Each of the 50 rooms in this former convent is furnished in a different English style, the most beautiful being the "pretty" room and the two suites. Even those used to being spoilt will find that this luxurious hotel, with its garden, tea salon, piano bar and excellent restaurant, leaves nothing to be desired. The hotel is situated in the upper city between the EU offices district and the city park. Rooms from Bfr 9,900. *Rue du Commerce, 9, Tel. 506 91 11, Fax 512 17 08, Metro: Arts-Loi*

boasts the luxury of having its own small garden. The fact that the atmosphere is always friendly is thanks to its Swedish owner. The hotel has 51 rooms and is situated in a quiet area on the Parc du Cinquantenaire. *Avenue de l'Yser 21–22, Tel. 735 74 00, Fax 735 19 67, Metro: Merode*

Le Plaza **(107/E2)**
City palace with a massive façade in the style of the 1930s, restored to its former glory. A favourite hotel of actors and musicians. *193 rooms, Boulevard Adolphe Max 118–126, Tel. 227 67 00, Fax 227 67 20, Metro: Rogier*

Plaza Crowne **(107/F2)**
Following a long period of renovation, this traditional hotel has now been restored to its former glory. This is where Prince Rainier and Grace Kelly stayed on their honeymoon. This was Brussels' first concrete building. Furnished in art nouveau style, it has 358 individually designed rooms. *Rue Gineste 3. Tel. 203 62 00, Fax 203 55 55, Metro: Rogier*

Sheraton Airport **(U/D3)**
A modern, comfortable airport hotel. Passengers can check in directly opposite. *299 rooms, Brussels National Airport, Tel. 725 10 00, Fax 725 11 55, airport train from Gare Centrale–Zaventem*

HOTELS CATEGORY 2

(for travellers with moderate expectations, double rooms between Bfr 4,800 and 8,000)

Art Hotel Siru **(107/F1)**
An extraordinary house situated in the vicinity of the north station, and not far from the centre of the city. The 101 rooms are not large, but they are comfortable and inspiring. All the rooms have an individual atmosphere and have been decorated by Belgian artists, sculptors and photographers to their own designs. The whole hotel, from the breakfast room, via the staircase to the brasserie, exudes artistic creativity. *Place Rogier 1, Tel. 203 35 80, Fax 203 33 03, Metro: Rogier, tram: 90*

Astrid **(107/E2)**
Pleasant new hotel opened in 1994 with every modern comfort; good value for money. *100 rooms, Place du Samedi, 11, Tel. 219 31 19, Fax 219 31 70, Metro: De Brouckère, Ste-Catherine*

Atlas **(107/D3)**
Situated in the middle of the old quarter. This friendly city hotel has only recently been built and has been furnished in a chic "designer" style. Weekend discounts. *88 rooms, rue du Vieux-Marché-aux-Grains 30–34, Tel. 502 60 06, Fax 502 69 35, Metro: Bourse*

Auberge Saint Michel **(107/E4)**
This narrow hotel is hidden behind the gilded façade of the Maison des Duc de Brabant. The simple furnishings of its 15 rooms may disappoint those with high expectations, but they will be amply compensated by having a view over the Grand' Place. *Grand' Place 15, Tel. 511 09 56, Fax 502 46 00, Metro: Gare Centrale*

Daystar **(104/A6)**
Comfortable hotel with contemporary furnishings. *49 rooms,*

Square Victoria 9, Tel. 219 06 61, Fax 219 38 82, Metro: Gare du Nord

Dôme I & II **(107/F2)**
★ Besides having a highly recommended restaurant, this hotel recalls the age of the "golden twenties". Restored in the style of the *belle époque*, it appeals especially to travellers who appreciate style. The original part of the building dates from 1902, and there is a new wing, also furnished with style, but more mordern. Central location, good brasserie. *125 rooms, Boulevard du Jardin Botanique 12–14, Tel. 218 06 80, Fax 218 41 12, Metro: Rogier*

Manos **(111/F2)**
★ A small, friendly house situated in the upper city, furnished in rustic style. One of the city's few intimate hotels with its own garden. If you want one of the best rooms, ask for one overlooking the garden. 38 spacious and well equipped rooms, also suitable for a fairly long stay. *Chaussée de Charleroi 100-104, Tel. 537 96 82, Fax 539 36 55, tram: 91, 92.*

Président Centre **(108/B3)**
★ A modern 73 room hotel in the heart of the city. All the rooms are well furnished but not over luxurious. The staff are friendly and helpful. *Rue Royale 160, Tel. 219 00 65, Fax 218 09 10, tram: 92, 93, 94*

HOTELS CATEGORY 3

(simple standards, double rooms between Bfr 1,550 and 4,800)

Agenda **(112/A3)**
A small, modern hotel in the shopping district not far from the Avenue Louise. The rooms have kitchenettes. Especially popular with Japanese and Italian tourists. *38 rooms, rue de Florence 6, Tel. 539 00 31, Fax 539 00 63, tram: 93, 94*

Albert Premier **(107/F2)**
A hotel for people who love the pace of city life. The rooms are modern with art deco style furnishings. The hotel has 285 rooms and its guests come from all over the world. It is especially popular with people travelling in a group. *Place Rogier 20, Tel. 203 31 25, Fax 203 43 31, Metro: Rogier*

Argus **(108/A6)**
Standing in the centre of the upper city's finest shopping streets, this hotel has 41 rooms. The service is polite – the rooms are rather small. July–Aug special prices. *Rue Capitaine Crespel 6, Tel. 514 07 70, Fax 514 12 22, Metro: Louise*

Balladins **(100/B3)**
A pleasant hotel, situated at the edge of the city not far from the Parc de Laeken and the Atomium. Suitable for motorists. Weekend arrangements. *49 rooms, Avenue Houba de Strooper, Tel. 476 15 14, Fax 476 13 96, Metro: Houba-Brugmann*

Les Bluets **(111/E2)**
★ If you are a non-smoker, and you do not mind the colour pink, then this is possibly the right address for you, and a bargain at this price. In the more prosperous part of the city, only a few minutes away from Avenue Louise with its high-class shops, this family hotel has eleven rather small rooms. Breakfast is served in the elegant drawing room. The

house also has a veranda. *Rue Berckmans 124, Tel. 534 39 83, Fax 534 09 70, Metro: Louise*

Du Congrès (108/B3)
This pleasant 52 room hotel is situated in a quiet part of the city not far from the rue Royale, and has especially impressive, lush flower arrangements. The rooms are a bit on the small side, but tastefully furnished and the service cannot be faulted. 15 minutes' walk from the centre. *Rue du Congrès 42–44, Tel. 217 18 90, Fax 217 18 97, Metro: Madou, tram: 92, 93, 94*

George V (106/C3)
A fine mansion dating from 1859, with 22 simple rooms, painted in pastel colours, and each large enough for up to four people. No.15 is the most comfortable. Quiet and centrally situated. Simple breakfast. *Rue t'Klint 23, Tel. 513 50 93, Fax 513 44 93, Metro: Bourse*

A la Grande Cloche (107/D4–5)
You will scarcely find better value in Brussels. Reasonably priced, clean and the atmosphere of the old Brussels: a little bit shabby, but then it is near the Marolles district. *37 rooms, Place Rouppe 10–12, Tel. 512 61 40, Fax 512 65 91, Metro: Anneessens*

Ibis off Grand-Place (107/F4)
One of several hotels situated in the historical centre of the city. The Ibis hides behind a (newly

Allow yourself to be spoilt for once, in the Hotel Astoria

erected) historical clinker façade. The interior is modern and convenient, the rooms small but light, some of them designed for three people. Very popular for group travel, which often makes for a somewhat hectic atmosphere. Unfriendly service, however the station is very near. *180 rooms, rue du Marché-aux-Herbes 100, Tel. 514 40 40, Fax 514 50 67, Metro: Gare Centrale*

La Légende **(107/E4)**
Small, simple city hotel not far from the Grand' Place. Built around a peaceful inner courtyard. Not all the 45 rooms have their own bathroom, but there is a shower and WC on each floor. There are also rooms for three, at favourable rates. *Rue du Lombard 35, Tel. 512 82 90, Fax 512 34 93, Metro: Bourse, Gare Centrale*

La Madeleine **(107/E4)**
Conveniently situated for all the city's activities. A very plain, simple hotel. *52 rooms, rue de la Montagne 22, Tel. 513 29 73, Fax 502 13 50, Metro: Gare Centrale, tram: 92, 93, 94*

Sabina **(108/B3)**
A simple, quietly situated 24 room hotel, charging reasonable prices. Especially popular with people attending conferences, many of whom stay here regularly. *Rue du Nord 78, Tel. 218 26 37, Fax 219 32 39, Metro: Madou*

Saint Nicolas **(107/E3)**
Centrally situated guesthouse, representing the best value to be found in the city centre. Simple family hotel. *60 rooms, rue du Marché-aux-Poulets 32, Tel. 219 04 40, Fax 219 17 21, Metro: Bourse*

Rembrandt **(112/A2)**
Plush family hotel with 10 bright, comfortable rooms. A corner house in a quiet situation in the upper city. *Rue de la Concorde 42, Tel 512 71 39, Fax 511 71 36, Metro: Louise*

Vendôme **(107/E2)**
★ Friendly hotel in the vicinity of the Place de Brouckère. The rooms are spacious and bright and the service is friendly. In spite of the fact that the hotel has 106 rooms, you are made to feel like an individual. *Boulevard Adolphe-Max 98, Tel. 227 03 00, Fax 218 06 83, Metro: De Brouckère, Rogier*

Welcome **(107/E2)**
★ One of Brussels' very small but fine hotels. Guests are treated as individuals, something for romantics. The house lies in the Ste-Cathérine district, with its excellent fish restaurants. *6 rooms, rue du Peuplier 5, Tel. 219 95 46, Fax 217 18 87, Metro: Ste-Catherine*

Windsor **(107/D4–5)**
The traditional building has recently been renovated, and the standard of the rooms improved accordingly; they are now bright and comfortable. The hotel lies ten minutes from the Grand' Place, and has a view of Brussels' most exclusive restaurant "Comme Chez Soi". *34 rooms, Place Rouppe 13, Tel. 511 20 14, Fax 514 09 42, Metro: Anneessens*

TRAVELLING WITH CHILDREN

Brussels hospitality does not just ensure that you will get good value for money, children are also made very welcome, and in many hotels extra beds for children (up to the age of 12) will be placed in double rooms at no extra charge.

JUST LIKE HOME

It is typical of Brussels hospitality that you will also find private houses offering bed and breakfast. *New Windrose* acts as an agency for such accommodation not only in Brussels but throughout Belgium. Prices begin at Bfr 1,600 for a double room with breakfast. The organisation also offers a service for introducing tourists to residents of Brussels, and arranges tours of the city. Only suitable if your stay is going to be relatively long. Reservations: *New Windrose, Avenue Paul-Dejaer 21A, B-1060 Brussels, Tel. 534 71 91, Fax 534 71 92*

FOR YOUNG PEOPLE

Auberge Bruegel **(107/E5)**
This youth hostel, which has 125 beds, is behind historic walls in the centre, ten minutes from the Gare Centrale. There are rooms for two or four people, as well as larger dormitories. Comfortable lounge and modern self-service restaurant. The most important places of interest are within walking distance. Single room Bfr 695, Bfr 570 for one person in a four-bed room. Members pay Bfr 100 less. *Rue du Saint-Esprit 2, Tel. 511 04 36, Fax 512 07 11, Metro: Gare Centrale*

Auberge Jacques Brel **(108/B2)**
French is the language mainly spoken here. Prices per person: single room Bfr 695, sharing a double room Bfr 570, or in a larger dormitory for 6 to 14, Bfr 410. *Rue de la Sablonnière 30, Tel. 218 01 87, Fax 217 20 05, Metro: Botanique*

Auberge La Fonderie **(106/B-C2)**
Pleasant hostel offering single rooms or dormitories for up to 12 people. Prices per person: single room Bfr 695, sharing a double room Bfr 570, or in a larger dormitory for 6 to 12, Bfr 410. *Rue de l'Eléphant 4, Sint-Jans-Molenbeek, Tel. 410 38 58, Fax 410 39 05, Metro: Comte de Flandre*

Bed & Brussels **(113/D4)**
This organisation acts as an agency for private accommodation. Bed and breakfast between Bfr 1,200 and 1,500. Reservations: *rue Victor Greyson 58, Tel. 646 07 37, Fax 644 01 14*

Le Centre Vincent van Gogh (CHAB Hostel) **(108/B2)**
A 210 bed hotel with a good reputation, friendly staff and a relaxed atmosphere. It is situated in the Schaerbeek quarter, opposite *Au Travers,* one of the best jazz clubs in the city. Prices per person: sharing a double room Bfr 570, single room about Bfr 700. There are also some rooms with four beds. Bar, restaurant. *Rue Traversière 8, Tel. 217 01 58, Fax 219 79 95, Metro: Botanique*

Sleep Well **(107/F2)**
Modern, light, centrally situated. Very good value for money, but not lacking in the usual hotel facilities, such as a bar *(closed Sun)* and restaurant (Belgian cuisine at moderate prices). There is also an Internet café which serves as a meeting point and information exchange. The room furnishings are functional. Double room about Bfr 577. *Rue du Damier 23, Tel. 218 50 50, Fax 218 13 13, Metro: Rogier*

Brussels diary

Festivals, fairs, the historical "Ommegang" and music competitions – in Brussels celebrations are both cosmopolitan and restrained

The people of Brussels always like to celebrate, and almost all their festivals can be traced back to a religious origin. The most important festival of the year is the Ommegang which takes place in July. First celebrated in 1549 by the city magistrate in the absence of Emperor Charles V, this has been the largest costume festival held by the city ever since and attracts countless numbers of visitors. A magnificently colourful procession files past against the historical backdrop of the city hall and the guildhalls, with mayors and guilds, the Queen of Austria, Christina of Denmark, and countless princes, bishops and counts – some of them represented by the descendants of great noble dynasties that were once famous. Those also taking part include the emperor's court, the members of the Order of the Golden Fleece, and hundreds of others – all in original costumes. The word *ommegang* is of Flemish origin and means, roughly "to walk round in procession". The first mention of the ommegang dates from 1348, when according to legend, a picture of the Virgin Mary was carried around the church in Sablon (or Zavel, to give it its Flemish name). In 1549 the city laid on the first ommegang for Emperor Charles V. In September the "Bruzzle", the festival of the Flemish community, is held. This Brussels festival promises to become a great international festival of culture. Its competitor is the summer festival of the French speaking residents – a healthy rivalry exists between the two cultural and linguistic communities. In the summer classical concerts are held in the Bois de la Cambre and in the Halles de Scherbeek, the old market halls "summer happenings".

Many activities and events take place in the summer months, above all on the Grand' Place, for example the spectacular *Son et Lumière* presentations. In the year 2000 Brussels is the "Cultural Capital of Europe", and the theme of "city" has been chosen to run through all its events.

The "Ommegang" festival goes back over 450 years

PUBLIC HOLIDAYS

1st January *(New Year)*, Easter Monday, 1st May *(Labour Day)*, Ascension Day, Whit Monday, 21st July *(Belgian National Celebration Day)*, 15th August

MARCO POLO SELECTION: EVENTS

1 Bruegel Festival
Traditional celebrations are held all over the old city (page 79)

2 Klinkende Munt
The Flemish celebrate their own culture (page 79)

3 Monument Days
Some 75 architectural monuments open their doors to the public (page 79)

4 Ommegang
Costume festival with a tradition going back 450 years (page 79)

5 Hothouses
Flowers in splendour in the glass city, open for just a few days (page 78)

6 Christmas Market
Traditional market with a commercial and cultural basis (page 79)

(Assumption Day), 1st November *(All Saints Day)*, 11th November *(Armistice Day)*, Christmas Day and Boxing Day.
If a public holiday falls on a Sunday, the following Monday is a holiday.

SPECIAL EVENTS

January
Motor Show (even years)
Cinema Festival in the Palais des Congrès (**108/B3**)
Antiques Fair in the Palais des Beaux-Arts (**107/F4**)

February
Carnival is celebrated with wild abandon in the city centre, especially on Shrove Tuesday

March
International Fantasy Film Festival (Auditorium 44)

April–September
Son-et-Lumière Performances on the Grand' Place, April–September daily at approximately 10–11 pm (**107/E4**)

April
★ The royal *hothouses* in Laeken (**100/F4**) are open to the public for about a week at the end of April and beginning of May

May
Queen Elisabeth International Music Competition in the Palais des Beaux-Arts and the Conservatoire (**107/F4**), *Tel. 507 82 00*
Brussels Jazz Marathon: Non-stop jazz is played in the pubs and on the squares, including the Grand' Place for three days and three nights (end of May–June, Tel. 456 04 85)

June
Brussels' *20 km run* – with folk festival character
The famous *Battle of Waterloo* is re-enacted as a grand spectacle (**U/C6**)
Kirmes in Tervuren (**U/D4**)
Flower Show in the Botanique (**108/B2**)
Music recitals with classical instruments every evening on the Grand' Place (**107/E4**)

July
Beginning of July: traditional ★ *Ommegang* on the Grand' Place (**107/E4**). Reserve seats at the Tourist Office in good time!
Beginning of July: ★ *Klinkende Munt: International Art-Festival* on the Place de la Monnaie (**107/E–F3**), *Tel. 513 82 90*
Every Sunday: *Classical concerts* or *Jazz* in the Bois de la Cambre (**U/C5**) *(11 am–1 pm, also in August and October)*
21 July: Numerous festivities in connection with the *National Celebration Day,* fireworks in Warande city park (**O**)
End of July–beginning of August: large annual market, *Foire du Midi,* at the south station (**106/C5**)

August
1st Sunday in August: *Putting up the Meyboom* (maypole), rue du Marain (**107/E4**), commemoration of a turbulent wedding that took place in 1213
Last two weeks of August: *Bellone-Brigittines*: seven performances on the themes of light, colour, and the moment
Carpet of flowers on the Grand' Place (**107/E4**), every even year (e.g. 2000)

September
Brabant Kirmes on the Grand' Place (**107/E4**)
★ *Bruegel Festival* in the old city
Gastronomical and Folk Festival in the Illôt Sacré (**107/E3**)
★ *Monument Days.* On the second weekend some 75 buildings open their doors, and there are guided tours, led by experts, across squares, through districts of the city and around buildings
Botanical Nights in the botanical gardens (Song Festival) (**108/B2**) *Tel. 226 12 11*

December
★ 2nd weekend *Christmas Market,* Grand' Place (**107/E4**)

Colourful summer spectacle: the enormous carpet of flowers on the Grand' Place

MIX'ORt

Out on the town

World-famous opera, crowded discos, jam sessions and plenty of pubs offer a huge variety of fun and enjoyment

The Royal Symphony Orchestra, the National Opera and the Concerts held in the *Palais des Beaux-Arts* are certainly famous. The trouble is, they are so popular that it is difficult to get hold of tickets. In the evenings the many bars, cafés, pubs and jazz taverns are cramped and stuffy. Numerous events are held every evening. Publications such as "Kiosque", which appears monthly, and the informative English-language "Bulletin" make it easier to choose what you want to do. Tickets should be ordered early (from TIB or OPT: see Information). Suitable clothing should be worn to concerts and the opera, and even for discos the appropriate dress code should be observed. Most of the cafés are situated around the Grand' Place, on the Place Saint-Géry, around the Grand Sablon, in the Marolles district and near the Stock Exchange. In the Congo quarter there are exotic and African establishments near the Naamse Poort. One thing you should bear in mind is that the public transport system closes at midnight.

The old hothouses of the former botanical gardens were turned into a centre for French culture in 1984

BARS/CAFÉS

The pubs of Brussels, known as *stamenei*, are a world of their own with a very special ambience. Most of the *Kroegen,* as the bars or pubs are called, are traditional establishments with highly polished tables, friendly service and a large selection of local beers, gins, and champagnes. To prevent misunderstanding, the term "café" is used to refer, not so much to somewhere selling coffee and cakes, as to a pub which also sells coffee. The terms "cafeteria" and "salon de thé" are roughly equivalent to "café" and "tea shop" in English.

A la Mort Subite **(107/F3)**

In this bar, whose name means "sudden death", beer is taken very seriously. This elongated bar, which has all the charm of a station pub, is where cultivated beer drinkers get together. At lunchtime and in the evening you will be luck to find a seat. Clerks, lobbyists and tourists make themselves at home on the wooden chairs to enjoy Kriek, Gueuze and Lambic beer. *Open daily 10 am–1 am, rue Montagne-aux-Herbes-Potagères 7, Metro: Gare Centrale*

L'Archiduc **(107/D3)**
With its genuine Art Deco interior, this is undoubtedly a favourite meeting place for those involved in the Brussels fashion and PR scene. *Open daily 4 pm–4 am, rue Dansaert 6, Metro: Bourse*

La Bécasse **(107/E3)**
The tables are well scrubbed, the atmosphere noisy, and the beer is Timmermans Lambic. The ham sandwiches are a speciality of the house. *Open daily 10 am–1 am, Sun from 11 am, rue de Tabora 11, Metro: Bourse*

Les Brasseurs **(107/E3)**
One of the few typical *brasseries* in Brussels. Simple, with wooden chairs. Beer, apéritifs and coffee are served. *Open daily from midday, Boulevard Anspach 77, Metro: Bourse*

Café Le Coq **(107/E3)**
This café is an institution, a meeting place for actors, down-and-outs, footballers and the merely curious. *Open daily 8 am–4 am, rue A. Orts, Metro: Bourse*

Chaloupe d'Or **(107/E4)**
★ The waiters run around like an Olympic sprinter. The pub is cluttered with traditional furnishings. Very mixed clientele, including Japanese tourists who like to have their photographs taken here in this typical Brussels brasserie. *Open daily from 9 am, until the last customer has paid. Grand' Place 24–25, Metro: Gare Centrale*

Chez Richard **(107/E5)**
The focus of night life around the *Grand Sablon*. Definitely the place to be seen. *Open daily from 8 pm until the early morning. rue des Minimes 4, tram 92, 93, 94*

Chez Moeder Lambic **(111/D4)**
The beer list is positively encyclopaedic, with about 1050 vari-

MARCO POLO SELECTION: NIGHT-LIFE

1 **Botanique**
Theatre, films and plenty of culture for francophiles (page 86)

2 **Who's Who Land**
Fun techno temple with guaranteed tropical atmosphere (page 84)

3 **Kladaradatsch**
Popular film palace with an atmospheric tavern (page 85)

4 **Chaloupe d'Or**
Stylish beer tavern, also serving Champagne (page 82)

5 **Théâtre Royal de la Monnaie**
The best stage presentations in the country (page 86)

6 **Palais des Beaux-Arts**
An acoustically exciting concert hall, built by Victor Horta (page 86)

7 **Théâtre Toone VII**
Puppet plays in the best Brussels tradition (page 87)

8 **Ultième Hallucinatie**
Elegant place of retreat for night owls and the fashionable young (page 83)

eties for the tireless drinker to choose from. Guests can also pass the time leafing through the comic books provided. *Open daily 4 pm–3 am, rue de Savoie 68, Metro: Albert, Horta*

Cirio **(107/E3)**
The comfortable atmosphere of an upper-middle-class drawing room at the turn of the 19th/20th centuries. Furnishings – and urinals! – from the *belle époque*, genteel ladies chat over the Gueuze beer, young people drink coffee, and the waiters are friendly in a fatherly sort of way. *Open daily from 10 am, rue de la Bourse 18, Metro: Bourse*

Dali's Bar **(107/E3)**
Dark blue and surrealistic, décor and music up to the 1960s. *Open daily 4 pm until sunrise, Petite Rue des Bouchers 25, Metro: Bourse*

Dolle Mol **(107/E4)**
This is the centre for Flemish cosmopolitans, a place where revolutions are planned and called off. The pub has a loyal clientele and a friendly atmosphere. *Open daily 11 am–1 am, Sat and Sun from 5 pm, rue des Éperonniers 52, Metro: Gare Centrale*

Falstaff **(107/E3)**
A legend and an institution. This classical *belle époque* café, which is under a preservation order, was closed down in spring 1999, due to tax debts. The Parisian entrepreneur, Sami Bouzide, came to the rescue by buying into the concern. In the "new" Falstaff, everything is a bit more expensive, but the old splendour remains, as it does in the *Montecristo* next door. *Open daily 9 am–4 pm, rue Henri Maus 17–25, Metro: Bourse*

Java **(107/D3)**
Flemish café, occasionally with live music. *Open Mon–Sat 3 pm–3 am, rue St Géry 14, Metro: Bourse*

Kafka **(107/E3)**
A meeting place for progressive café customers. Vodka is also enjoyed here, with 13 different varieties being available. Jazz and blues provide the entertainment. *Open Mon–Fri from 10.30 pm, Sat from 5 pm–5 am, Sun 7 pm–2 am, rue de la Vierge Noire 6–8, Metro: De Brouckère*

A Malte **(111/E2)**
This really is a must for any visitor to Brussels, whether by daylight or candlelight. Wide brunch menu, garden. *Open daily 10 am–3 pm, rue Berckmans 30, Metro: Louise*

Ultième Hallucinatie **(104/B6)**
★ This art nouveau style showpiece is furnished with wooden benches from old railways. In 1904 the building was established as the residence of the noble family Cohn-Donnay. For years it has been used as a meeting place not only for the fashionable young, but also for students of architecture and night owls. *Open daily from 11 am, Sat from 4 pm, rue Royale 316, Metro: Botanique*

Vieux Spijtigen Duivel **(110/C6)**
Reputed to be the oldest beer house in the city. According to legend, Emperor Charles V slaked his thirst here in the days when the hostelry was known as "The Angel". However, the Emperor was so unimpressed

with the unfriendly service, that he had the name changed to *Spijtigen Duivel* ("Angry Devil"). Genuine pub culture. *Open daily 11.30 am–1.30 am, Chaussée d'Alsemberg 621*

DISCOS & CLUBS

Before eleven o'clock in the evening there is nothing much going on in the discos. The choice is not great, but the ones that do exist are among the top class in Europe. Admission from Bfr 300.

Le Grain d'Orge **(108/C5)**
Generations of smokers have turned the paintwork brown in this music café where jazz and blues are played on Friday. *Open Tue–Sun 11 am–3 am, Chaussée de Wavre 142, Tel. 511 26 47, Metro: Porte de Namur*

Machado **(107/E4)**
Salsa and samba, Latin American music predominates here. Lots of atmosphere. *Open daily from 11 pm, rue des Chapeliers 14, Tel. 511 36 91, Metro: Gare Centrale*

Le Mambo **(108/C4)**
There is a pronounced African feel to this club with its somewhat eccentric music and exotic atmosphere.
Open Fri, Sat and Sun from 10 pm, Chaussée de Wavre 70, Tel. 513 55 29, Metro: Porte de Namur

Le Mirano Continental **(108/C3)**
Converted cinema with plenty of chrome and sparkle. The best looking young people in Brussels meet in this modern disco. To be allowed in, you need to have that certain something! *Open Sat 11 pm–5 am, Tel. 218 57 72, Chaussée de Louvain 38, Metro: Madou*

La Movida **(107/D3)**
Tapas and Flamenco and very Andalusian, with a fantastic atmosphere at weekends. *Open Tue–Sun from 7 pm, rue St-Géry, Tel. 502 02 84, Metro: Bourse*

Le Sud **(107/E3)**
The floors of this café, which consists of numerous rooms, are covered with worn Persian carpets; the décor is Arabian, the atmosphere Bohemian. One of Brussels most fashionable clubs. *Open Tue–Sat 10 am–6 am, rue de l'Écuyer 43, Metro: De Brouckère*

Tour & Taxi **(102/D–E5)**
High-tech dance club, with progressive music. Admission free before midnight. Gloomy surrounding area, so take a taxi. *Open Fri–Sat 11 pm–5 am, rue Picard 5, Metro: Belgica*

Who's Who Land **(107/D5)**
★ This "techno temple" has a strong appeal for the latex generation. Several floors of noise and fun. Thursday is rap and reggae night. Admission Bfr 300. *Thu–Sat 11 pm–6 am, rue du Poincon, Metro: Anneessens*

JAZZ

Bierodrome **(112/B2)**
This club is the base for a lively jazz scene, with traditional jazz figuring prominently. *Tue–Thu midday–3 am, Fri–Sun 4 pm–3 am, Place Fernand Cocqu 21, Tel. 512 04 56, bus: 51, 74*

Sounds **(112/B1)**
Small café with high-quality jazz.

Jazz, Jazz, Jazz

Open Tue–Sun from 6 pm, rue de la Tulpe, Tel. 218 40 86, Metro: Port de Namur

Travers **(108/B2)**
Lovers of jazz and experimental music congregate here every evening. *Rue Traversière 11, Tel. 218 40 86, Metro: Botanique*

Zebra Bar **(107/D3)**
Although jazz is not regularly played here, it is a good place to relax and enjoy a cocktail – on the pavement if the weather is fine. *Open daily 11.45 am–2.30 am (Fri and Sat until 3 am), Place-St-Géry 33–35, Tel. 511 09 01, Metro: Bourse*

CINEMA

The films shown at the majority of cinemas are always subtitled, mostly in French and Dutch as they are usually English-language films. The advantage of this is that all the films shown in the cinemas are in the original version. The films currently showing are listed in the daily newspapers, with "Le Soir" and "Belgique Numéro Un" providing the most detail. Tickets cost about Bfr 250, somewhat less on Mondays.

Arenberg-Galeries **(107/E3)**
Art deco, plush seating, but showing the most up-to-date international films. *Galeries Saint-Hubert 26, Tel. 512 80 63, Metro: Gare Centrale*

Kinepolis **(100/C3)**
Multiplex with 26 auditoriums and Imax projection on a 600 sq m screen. Films in French, English and Dutch. *Bruparck, for programme Tel. 0900/352 41, Metro: Heysel*

Kladaradatsch Palace **(107/E3)**
★ ⊙ Art deco film palace, carefully restored, three cinemas, comfortable family atmosphere

Son et Lumière on the Grand' Place

The King's house, which was never lived in by a king, and was once used by the bakers as their guildhall is bathed in light, together with the Gothic city hall and the magnificent façades of the old guildhalls. Between April and September the Grand' Place is lit up whilst the music of Mozart or Schubert is heard from loudspeakers. The Son-et-Lumière shows begin as darkness falls; between the beginning of April and the end of September the spectacle takes place at between 10.30 pm and 11 pm, in summer between 10.45 pm and 11.15 pm.

in the bar. *Boulevard Anspach 85, Metro: Bourse*

Musée du Cinéma **(107/F4)**
A particularly beautiful cinema in which old silent films and classical films are shown daily. Book in advance. *Open daily from 5.30 pm, rue Baron Horta 9, Tel. 507 83 70, Metro: Gare Centrale*

UGC De Brouckère **(107/E2)**
With ten screens, this is one of the largest cinemas in the city. *Information Tel. 0900/104 40, Place de Brouckère, Metro: De Brouckère*

CONCERTS/OPERA

Countless spectacular productions have helped to make the *Opera*, and the *Théâtre Royale de la Monnaie* (*Koninklijke Muntschouwburg* in Flemish) famous far beyond Belgium's national boundaries. Concert-goers and opera lovers who want a detailed programme should contact the organisation *Balconop, rue Marché-aux-Herbes 63, 1000 Brussels, Tel. 504 03 90, Fax 513 69 50*

Botanique **(108/B2)**
★ Classical concerts, jazz, theatre, films and plenty of culture. *Rue Royale 236, Tel. 226 66 60, Metro: Botanique*

Cirque Royal **(108/B3)**
Palace of culture with 3,000 seats and good acoustics. Rock and jazz concerts. *Rue de l'Enseignement 81, Tel. 218 20 15, tram: 29, 63, Metro: Madou*

Conservatoire Royal de la Musique **(108/A5)**
Classical concerts performed by the *conservatoire*'s own symphony orchestra or a visiting ensemble. *Rue de la Régence 30, Tel. 507 82 00, tram: 92, 93, 94*

Les Halles de Schaerbeek **(104/C4)**
Former indoor market halls, now completely renovated to provide a venue for numerous cultural events. *Rue Royale-Ste-Marie 22, Tel. 218 00 31, tram: 92, 93, 94*

Palais des Beaux-Arts **(107/F4)**
★ The Henry-Le-Bœuf hall is one of the best concert halls in the whole world, an acoustic masterpiece by the art deco architect Victor Horta. Lunchtime concerts are held on Tuesdays at 12.40 pm from January to April. (no telephone bookings). *Rue Ravenstein 23, Tel. 507 82 00, Metro: Gare Centrale*

Théâtre Royal de la Monnaie **(107/E3)**
★ The performances directed by Gérard Mortier, who succeeded Herbert von Karajan at the Salzburg Festival, were among the most brilliant in Europe, with operatic and ballet performances gaining fame way beyond Belgium's national boundaries. There are tours of the building, with its classical façade and modern foyer, every Saturday at midday. *Place de la Monnaie, Tel. 229 12 11, Metro: De Brouckère*

THEATRES/THEATRE CAFÉS

Brussels is a wonderful place for lovers of stage shows and rejoices in a large number of theatres, more than two dozen in fact, catering for all kinds of drama presented in French, Dutch (Flemish) or Brussels dialect. A good seat will cost anywhere

The opera alone makes the trip worth while

between Bfr 700 and 1000. For reservations: *Tel. 0800/212 21*

Kaaitheater (107/D1)
Independent, trend-setting playhouse presenting numerous international co-productions, some of them in Flemish. *Sainctelettesquare 20, Tel. 201 59 59 and 201 58 58, Metro: Yser*

Koninklijke Vlaamse Schouwburg (107/E2)
Flemish-language theatre, presenting experimental and classical works. *Rue de Laeken 146, Tel. 217 69 37, Metro: Yser*

La Samaritaine (O)
Theatre café where chanson singers frequently appear. *Rue de la Samaritaine 16, Tel. 511 33 95, tram: 92, 93, 94*

Théâtre du Rideau de Bruxelles (107/F4)
Both new and classical works by Belgian authors are performed in this art deco palace of fine arts. *Rue Ravenstein 23, Tel. 507 83 60, Metro: Gare Centrale*

Théâtre Royale (107/E3)
The "Theatre Royal" dates back to 1847, and comedies figure prominently in its programme. *Galerie du Roi 32, Tel. 512 04 07, Metro: Gare Centrale*

Théâtre Royale du Parc (108/B4)
French-language theatre which specializes in showing the modern classics. *Rue de Loi 3, Tel. 512 23 39, Metro: Arts-Loi*

Théâtre Toone VII (107/E2)
★ Brussels' most famous puppet theatre. José Géal has remained faithful to a tradition of puppetry which goes back to the time of Philip II. The Spanish kings banned plays from the theatre because they often made fun of the occupying forces. Thus it came about that the roles were taken over by wooden figures. Farces in Brussels dialect are particularly popular. Historical tavern *Estaminet. Open Tue–Sat 8.30 pm, Petite Rue des Bouchers 21, Tel. 511 71 37, Metro: Gare Centrale, Bourse*

In touch with the real Brussels

These walking tours are marked in green on the map on the back cover and in the Street Atlas beginning on page 100

① WALL PAINTINGS: ON THE TRAIL OF WORLD-FAMOUS COMIC HEROES

On this walking tour through the lower city of Brussels you will encounter not only Bohemians but also famous heroes painted on the walls. Duration: about three hours.

Brussels has many places providing proof that surrealism exists in reality. And as the city is also the scene of numerous comic stories – like that of the Manneken Pis *(page 18)* in the "Black Tower", the Grand' Place for Suske and Wiske or the Galeries Saint-Hubert *(page 18)*, a campaign was initiated in the 1990s, to decorate grey walls with scenes from the most famous Belgian comics. It is intended that a new mural should be painted every year, so that eventually a walk through Brussels will become a comic-strip experience.

This walking tour which takes you past these wall paintings begins at the Grand' Place *(page 28)*. Leave the market place by the city hall through the little street rue de la Tête d'Or. which still retains something of the old city's charm. At No. 19 (opposite the police station) in the narrow rue du Marché-au-Charbon you can see Françoise Schulten's "*Les Pas Sages*". Then, if you cross the rue du Midi you will come to the *Plattesteen* where the wall of the house by the neat tavern with its large terrace is decorated with a charming mural by Frank Pé, entitled the *Broussaille,* showing two bright boys out for a walk.

Opposite the five-storey building with the green window frames stands the British journalist Victor Sackville, or at least a picture of him. This comic hero, created by Francis Carin, is involved in an espionage affair that actually took place in the city during the First World War. Just a short distance to the right, you will find yourself in the little street rue des Bon Secours where blonde hero Ric Hochet adorns the façade of a prominent old house. The journalist Ric, also known as Ric Ringers is here accompanied by Commissioner Bourdon, and is climbing on an imaginary gutter, to rescue Nadine, who is hanging out of a window and being harassed by a suspicious figure inside the house.

On the other side of the busy Boulevard Anspach, which passes through the old quarter and was modelled on its counterpart in Paris, cross the Place Fontainas and walk along the rue Anderlecht, which, it must be said, is in need of redevelopment, to the rue de la Buanderie. Here, in "Laundry Street", is the main attraction of all the murals: Lucky Luke, Jolly Jumper and the four Dalton brothers are shown in action, The Adventures of Lucky Luke, with some 270 million copies, are amongst the best selling European comic strips of all times.

The trail then leads to the right, in the direction of the Place du Jardin, then right again to the Six Jetons. Follow the rue des Riches Claires, then turn left to the Place Saint Géry, and the restored market halls, which date from 1881. Here you are in the oldest part of Brussels which is full of atmosphere and flair, and you will find numerous cafés and small bistros, where bohemian types cultivate an unorthodox lifestyle. To the left of the market halls you will see Nero, Marc Sleen's eponymous hero.

The comic heroes trail continues to the blackened façade of the church of St Catherine *(page 23)* and to the quai aux Briques with its many fish restaurants. Take the second turning into the Nom de Jésu, which leads through to the rue de Flandre. On the right you can see the strange character Cubitus of Dupa looking down, parodying in his own particular way the city's emblem the Mannemen Pis.

The tour now leads back in the direction of St Catherine's church across the square of the same name into the rue de Laeken. With its small shops, traditional beer houses and peeling façades this street still retains something of its original style. At the rue du Canal crossing, the most famous comic heroes in the country beckon: Suske and Wiske. This wall-painting, created in 1996 to mark Willy Valderstein's heroes' birthday, shows a familiar picture: Jerom holding up Lambik, who in turn has Aunt Sidonia on his shoulders – and Wiske and Suske right at the top.

The tour is rounded off by a visit to the Comic Centre. Go through the rue du Pont-Neuf in the direction of Boulevard Emile Jacqumain and Boulevard Adolphe Max, pass the lively shopping street rue Neuve, and you will come to the quiet, peaceful Place des Martyrs *(page 30)*. From here, passing between tall office buildings, it is not far to the centre of flourishing comic culture in the rue Sables. This, the largest and most beautiful museum of comics in Europe *(page 36)*, is situated in a former art nouveau department store, restored in 1989 at a cost of several millions. This was the Waucquez fabric store, built by the great art nouveau architect Victor Horta towards the end of the belle époque. No other city in the world has as many magnificent art nouveau buildings as Brussels. In the museum itself you can find out just about all there is to know about the history of the "ninth art", which is the name given to comics in Belgium, where stories told in pictures enjoy equal status with other narrative arts such as theatre, literature and film.

② JUBILEEE PARK AND A VISIT TO EUROPE IN THE "CHEESE BOX"

This tour leads to the "Jubilee Park" and through the lively district of Etterbeek to the glass palaces of the EU, at whose centre stands the "Cheese Box". You will see the traces left by a frenzy of constructional activity in the Leopold district. Duration: about three and a half to four hours.

If you come out of the Metro at the Point Schuman, you will be standing right in front of the European Union buildings: on the left, the Palais Berlaymont *(page 16)* which is still under wraps, and the imposing Justus Lipsius building – named after a philosopher from Brabant – towers up to the right. This is the seat of the EU Council of Ministers and thus provides jobs for some 2,500 EU employees and a whole army of journalists. Behind this, and only a stone's throw away, lies the luxurious complex Résidence Palace. After you have crossed the Rond-Point-Schuman you will see the European Bookshop at No. 244 in the rue de La Roi, where visitors interested in Europe will find all the reading material they could possibly wish for.

The walk then takes you to the Parc du Cinquantenaire ("Jubilee Park" – *page 40*), which is dominated by a magnificent triumphal arch. To mark the occasion of the fiftieth anniversary of Belgian independence, King Leopold II fulfilled his heart-felt desire to make Brussels a city that would be the equal of Paris. Boulevards were made through historical districts, parks laid out, and the Jubilee halls for the world exhibition of 1880 erected, although the architecturally splendid complex was not completed until 1905. Today the side wings house important museums: Autoworld, the historical museum and the military museum with their extensive collections. The park is dominated by 30 metre wide arches. It is in any case well worth climbing the 140 steps of the triumphal arc. In the shadow of the chariot statue, you will have a wonderful panoramic view over the city, the European district and the broad Avenue Tervuren, which leads to the royal domain of Tervuren, where the Royal Museum for Central Africa *(page 38)* is situated. The museums are a real treasure trove. However it is best to decide on just one to visit, as the abundance of the exhibits is simply overwhelming.

Next take the path along the right-hand wing (containing Autoworld) and strike off across the park along the first path you come to, towards the fountain, which will bring you out on the Avenue des Gaulois. Opposite, at No. 3 in the rue des Francs stands the Maison Cauchie, whose façade was decorated by the architect Paul Cauchie in 1905 in the style of the Pre-Raphaelites. Just a few steps further, at the bus stop on the Avenue des Gaulois, a flight of steps *(Mont du Cinquantenaire)* leads to the Chaussée Saint-Pierre in the Etterbeek district of the city, which still has some

No city visit is complete without seeing the Triumphal Arch

midday–5.45 pm; Acotra World (**107/E4**), *Magdalenasteenweg 51, Tel. 512 55* 40 (arranges overnight accommodation); *SOS Jeunes, for young people in need: Tel. 512 90 20*

LOST PROPERTY

Railway
For items lost on the train or in the station: *Tel. 555 25 55*
Airport
National Airport arrivals hall, Tel. 753 60 11, or visitors' hall, 1st floor, only on weekdays, Tel. 723 68 20 and 723 31 11
Metro, bus, tram
S.T.I.B. Lost Property Office, Avenue Toison d'Or, open weekdays 9.30 am–12.30 pm, Tel. 515 23 94

PARKING

There are a number of multi-storey car parks in the centre of Brussels. These are marked on the street atlas by means of a white "P" on a blue background. Charges: quarter of an hour costs Bfr 5, one hour Bfr 40. *Open Mon–Sat 9 am–7 pm.* Some multi-storey car parks shut at 10 pm and at the weekend.

POST

Postal charges abroad: *postcards Bfr 17, letters up to 20 g: Bfr 17 within the EU, otherwise Bfr 34*

Post offices are open Monday–Friday 9 am–5 pm, whilst the post office for Brussels X, *Avenue Fosny 48 A*, at the Gare du Midi is open 24 hours a day. Central post office: 1st floor in the Centre Monnaie: *Place de la Monnaie, also open Sat 9 am–3 pm*

PUBLIC TRANSPORT

The capital has a dense, well-developed system of public transport, consisting of trams, Metro, buses and taxis. The Metro network is 36 km long, and trains run between 6 am and midnight. Tickets can be bought at the ticket offices in the larger Metro stations or from ticket machines. Tickets must be cancelled before you commence your journey. Metro stopping places are designated by a large white "M" on a blue background, tram and bus stops by blue and white or red and white signs. At *"sur demande"* ("request") stops the driver will only stop if you raise your hand. The orange buses (S.N.C.V.) go out to the suburbs.

Single ticket Bfr 50
One-day ticket Bfr 130
Five-journey ticket Bfr 240
Ten-journey ticket Bfr 340

Information and timetables are provided free of charge, as is the interesting information sheet on "Art in the Metro".

Smoking is forbidden on all public transport and in all public buildings (station, post office and museums). The Brussels public transport system's information office *S.T.I.B.* is situated in the *Galeries de la Toison d'Or 20* (**111/E1**), *6th floor.*

TAXIS

Brussels taxi drivers are generally regarded as helpful and friendly. Compared with those in some other capital cities they are almost unbelievably pleasant. They like to be thought of as international, and make every effort to ensure mutual understanding. *The basic fare is Bfr 95 (surcharge of Bfr 75 at night); the per kilometre charge is Bfr 38 in the city centre or Bfr 76 outside the centre.* Taxi *Autolux Tel. 411 12 21, A.T.R.: Tel. 647 22 22, Taxis Orange: Tel. 513 62 00, Taxis Verts: Tel. 349 49 49*

Post your cards here!

TELEPHONE

Telephone cards in denominations of Bfr 200, 500 and 1,000 can be bought at post offices and newspaper kiosks. Coin-operated telephones take Bfr 5 and Bfr 20 coins.

Dialling code for *Britain: 00 44, USA and Canada: 00 1 followed by area code*, dialling code to Brussels from abroad: *0032/2,* national information: *14 07,* international: *14 04*

TIPPING

In Brussels, as elsewhere, tipping is customary. Cinema usherettes: *Bfr 20,* toilet attendants: *Bfr 10–20*, porters *Bfr 50*, hairdressers 20 percent of the charge. For taxi drivers you can round up the fare, but in restaurants you should only tip if the service was satisfactory.

TOURIST PASSPORT

With the tourist passport, which has more than 100 pages, is available from the tourist office for Bfr 300 and is valid for a year, you can save up to Bfr 1,000. Amongst other things the passport contains a one-day ticket for the public transport system, and gives reduced admission to about 40 museums – but is only worth buying for a fairly long stay.

WEIGHTS & MEASURES

1 cm	0.39 inch
1 m	1.09 yd (3.28 ft)
1 km	0.62 miles
1 sq m	1.20 sq yds
1 ha	2.47 acres
1 sq km	0.39 sq miles
1 g	0.035 ounces
1 kg	2.21 pounds
1 British	1016 kg
1 US ton	907 kg

1 litre is equivalent to 0.22 Imperial gallons and 0.26 US gallons

WHEN TO GO

Brussels has a moderate, Continental climate, with no season that is particularly wet or dry, as rainfall is evenly distributed throughout the year. In May, July and September the weather is regarded as fairly settled.

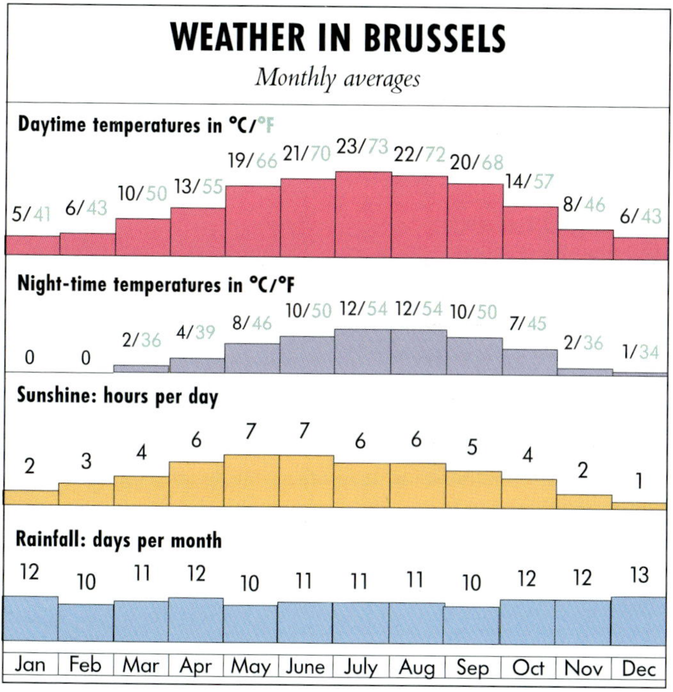

Do's and don'ts

A few things to be borne in mind when visiting Brussels

Station

As in most large cities, particular caution is advised in and around the stations and on the international trains – to Amsterdam or Paris. Keep an eye on your luggage, and in crowds take extra care of your money and papers. As in every other metropolis, there are pickpockets operating in the Metro and in places popular with tourists. In the evening it is best to avoid the area around the north and south stations, the city park and the Place Anneessens. At night it is not a good idea to travel alone on the Metro in the outlying districts if this can possibly be avoided.

The "Belly of Brussels"

The Ilôt Sacré district with its cobbled streets such as Petite Rue des Bouchers, Marché aux Fromage, Rue des Dominicains etc. is where you are most likely to be overcharged. This gastronomical red-light district entices tourists with displays of mussels and oysters on ice, sea urchins and lobsters, hare and venison – illuminated with red neon lights. Apart from half a dozen exceptions this area is dominated by the culinary Mafia. By all means stroll through these streets with their many restaurants, but try not to be seduced into eating there. If you do succumb however, make sure you check the bill. On Sundays many good restaurants are closed.

Etiquette

The first language is French, but a good deal of Flemish (Dutch) is also spoken. When you are trying to ask for something it helps if your questions are liberally interspersed with polite phrases. People tend not to be noisy in Brussels, even in pubs, and it is usual to queue at the ticket office, and at bus and tram stops. In shops and restaurants people wait quietly until it is their turn to be served. Pushing in is regarded as very impolite.

Dress

Visitors who run around in tracksuits, trainers or sandals cannot hope to make a good impression; beach clothes are considered not the thing in the city. In Brussels clothes that are casual but elegant are popular, and for concerts, hotels, elegant restaurants or discos, it is important to observe the appropriate dress code in each case.

Cycling

Discovering Brussels by bicycle is definitely not a good idea.. There are practically no cycle routes and far too much traffic for cycling to be safe or pleasant.

Street Atlas of Brussels

Please refer to back cover for an overview of this Street Atlas

250 m
A
B
C
1
2
3
4
5
6
HEYSEL/HEIZEL
WEMMEL
R0
Romeinse-steenweg
Chaussée Romaine
Van der Vekenstr.
Fabiolaln.
Laeken-veld
Panoramastr.
Kon. Elisabeth-ln.
Burvenich-ln.
R.du Cresson Waterkersstr.
Pl.du Lotus-pl.
R.d.l. Ciboulette
R. du Verregat
R.d.l. Sauge
R.des Genévriers
Chem. de Pourpier
R.des Pivoines
Av.des Magnolias
Magnolialn.
Av. de l'Héliport Helihavenln.
Av. des Grands Palais
Av. des Transports
Parc des Expositions
Tentoonstellingspark
Av. d.l. Science
Av. de Miramar-ln.
Av. des Beaux Arts
Pl. de Belgique Belgiëpl.
Pl. du Centenaire Eeuwfeestpl.
Av. Impératrice Charlotte
Keizerin Charlotte-laan
Heysel
Heizel
Bd. du Centenaire
Cité Modèle
Modelwijk
R. Baudouin
K. Boudewijn
Av. des Amandiers
Av. des Citronniers
Av. de Lima-ln.
Avenue Houba de Strooper-laan
Stade Roi Baudouin
Koning Boudewijnstadion
Av.des Athlètes
Av. du Championnat
Atomium
Bruparck
Mini-Europe
Planetarium
Av. du Football
Av. du Marathon
Av. de Bouchout
Boechoutln.
HEYS
Av. du Disque
Av. Gal. de Ceuninck
Sq. Palfijn
Jean Palfijn-ln.
Av. Joseph
Ste.Claire
Av. Emile Dekeyserln.
Sq.R. Alleinsq.
Av. Thiriar-ln.
Av. v.Ermengem-ln.
Bra-chet-ln.
Av. Laënnec-ln.
Av. Kufferath-ln.
Avenue Jean Baptiste Depaire-laan
Rue Stiénon
Pl.M. Tircher-pl.
Avenue de Heyn
Pl. G. Pattijn-pl.
Houba-Brugmann
Rue du Heysel
Rue Reper
Rommelaere-laan
Av. du Heymbosch
Av. V. Engeland-ln.
Rd.-Pt. d.l. Cité Jardin
Hôpital Brugmann
Brugmann Hospitaal
Bois de Dieleghem
Dielegemse-bos
Centre Sportif J.J.Crocq Sportcentrum
Av. Jean Joseph Crocq-ln.
R. Stuyvenberg-str.
Stuyvenbergh
Pl.A.Van Gehuchten-plein
Av. du Sacré Coeur
Rue Bonaventure-straat
Couvent du Sacré Cœur Klooster v.het H.Hart
Parc Roi Baudouin
Koning Boudewijnpark
Boulevard de Smet de Naeyer-laan
Av.du Compté de Jette Graafschap Jetteln.
Parc de la Jeunesse Jeugdpark
S.S.Anges H.H.Engelen
Rue Dupré-straat
Jette
Pl.Cardinal Mercier
St. Pierre St. Pieter
Cimetière de Jette Begraafplaats
102
100

BERGEN
A12
Boechout-ln.
Antwerpseln.
Nieuwe-Linde-ln.
Jozef Van Elewyck-str.
Klauwaarts-ln.
Luitberg
Bergdal
Heuveldal
Mormonenkerk
Strombeeklinde
Valkendal
Kasteelstr.
St. Annalaan
St. Annastr.
Mutsaard-pl.
Mutsaardstr.
Chaussée Romaine
Av. de l'Esplanade
Avenue de Madrid-laan
Avenue de Meysse
Meiseselaan
Av. de la Croix Rouge
Rode Kruisln.
Av. de l'Amphore
Amforaln.
Avenue du Forum
Forumlaan
Parc du Forum-park
Mutsaard-laan
Av. Wannecouter
Av. Demanet-str.
R. Gustave
Rue De Wand-straat
Petite ch. Romaine
R. Paul Janson-str.
Av. Jean de Bologne-ln.
Av. d.l. Brise
Briesln.
Av. de Bus
Bleydenln.
Avenue des Pagodes
Av. de l'Amarante
Av. de l'Atomium-laan
Parc d'Osseghem
Ossegem-park
Kreupelbosln.
Av. des Frondaisons
Loverlaan
Av. du Vieux Bruxelles
Oud Brusselln.
Av. des Coudriers
Hazelaarsln.
B.R.T.
Theatre de Verdure
Av. du Hallier
Av. Gros-Tilleul
Dikke-lindelaan
R21
LAEKEN
LAKEN
Pavil. Chinois
Chinees Pavil.
Statue J. de Bologne
Tour Japonaise
Japanse Tor
Parc de Laeken
Park van Laken
Avenue des Trembles
Av. des Pervenches
Maagdenpalmln.
Villa Belvédère
Monument Léopold I
Av. des Seringas
Pl. d.l. Dynastie
Vorstenhuis-pl.
Av. d.l. Dynastie
Vorstenhuislaan
Av. des Narcisses
Wildejasmijnenlaan
Avenue du Parc Royal
Serres Royales
Koninklijke Serres
feestln.
Pl. St. Lambert
St. Lambertus-pl.
Sacré Cœur et St. Lambert
Av. J. Sobieski-ln.
Château du Stuyvenberg
Stuyvenberg-kasteel
Avenue des Ebbebomenlaan
Chapelle Ste. Anne
Abelenlaan
Av. des Robiniers
Witte Acacialn.
Parc R. Elisabeth
K. Elisabeth Park
Sq. Clémentine-sq.
Ecole des Cadets
Kadettenschool
Rue Medori-str.
Drève Ste. Anne
St. Annadreef
Avenue Koninklijke
Parklaan
Château Royal
Koninklijk Kasteel
Domaine Royal de Laeken
Boulevard Emile Bockstael-laan
R. du Mt. St. Albansbergstraat
R. Alfred Stevens-str.
Ramaekers-str.
R. de Ter Plast-str.
R. des Horticulteurs
Tuinbouwers-str.
R. Karel Bogaerd-str.
R. des Chrysanthemes
R. de Vrière-str.
R. du Verdier
Sq. Pr. Charles
Kunstenaarsstr.
R. des Artistes
Sq. du Card. Cardijn
Cimetière
R. E. Van der Aa
Couronne
Bockstael
R. Fineau-str.
Kroonveld
Rue des Vignes
Wijngaardenstr.
R. M. Desmaré
BRUX

101

103

A
B
C
1
2
3
5
100
106
102
N290
JETTE
KOEKELBERG
Jeugdpark
Rue Dupré- straat
R. Antoine Baeck str.
Pl. Cardinal Mercier
St. Pierre St. Pieter
Cimetière de Jette Begraafplaats
Av. Secretin- ln
Parc Garcet
Av. de l'Exposition
Avenue de Laeken
Boulevard de Smet de Naeyer- ln.
Avenue Charles Woeste- ln.
Universelle Wereldtentoonstellings-
Pl. Reine Astrid
Rue Léopold I- straat
Ste. Madeleine
Av. de Jette
Jette- laan
Av. Broustin- ln.
Av. Carton de Wiart- ln.
Avenue des Gloires Nationales
Basilique du Sacré Cœur
Heilig-Hart-Basiliek
Av. J. Sermon- ln.
Av. E. Bossaert- ln.
Parc Elisabeth- park
Landsroemlaan
Av. du Panthéon
Simonis
Pl. E. Simonis
Boulevard
Av. de la Liberté
Vrijheids- ln.
Av. du Karreveld- ln.
Château du Karreveld
Kasteelhoeve van Karreveld
Stade Sippelberg Stadion
Chaussée de Gand
Gentsesteenweg
Osseghem
Ossegem
Zwarte Vijvers
Etangs Noirs
St. Charles Boromée
Ste. Anne St. Anna
250 m

D
E
F
101
103
107
1
2
3
4
5
6
Bockstael
Pannenhuys
Pannenhuis
Belgica
Ribaucourt
Yser
Ijzer
L A E K E N
Cimetière de Laeken
Begraafplaats van Laken
Gare de Tour et Taxis
Station van Turn en Taxis
Bassin Vergote
Bassin Beco
Parc Maximilien
Parc Maxi-milien-park
Bd. Emile Bockstael-ln.
Parklaan
Jubelfeestlaan
Belgica-ln.
Bd. du Jubilé
Leopold-II-laan
Rue Picard-str.
Avenue du Port
Havenlaan
Quai des Steamers
Quai de Willebroeck-kaai
Boulevard Bolivar
Allée Verte
Pl. des Armateurs
Redersplein
Léopold I-straat
Rue Marie-Christine
Maria-Christina
Steylsstraat
Pl. Emile Bockstael-pl.
Sq. des Combattans
Strijderssq.
Pl. M. DeMoor
Grotte N.D. de Lourdes
O.L.V.v.L.Grot
Parvis N.D.
O.L.V. voorpl.
Laeken
Maison Rouge
Pl. J.B. Willems
WTC
Pte. d'Anvers
Antwerpse-poort
Chaussée d'Anvers
Pl. et Sq. Sainctelette
Pl. de l'Yser
Ijzerpl.
l'Héliport
St. Remi
Sq. des Libérateurs
Bevrijders-sq.

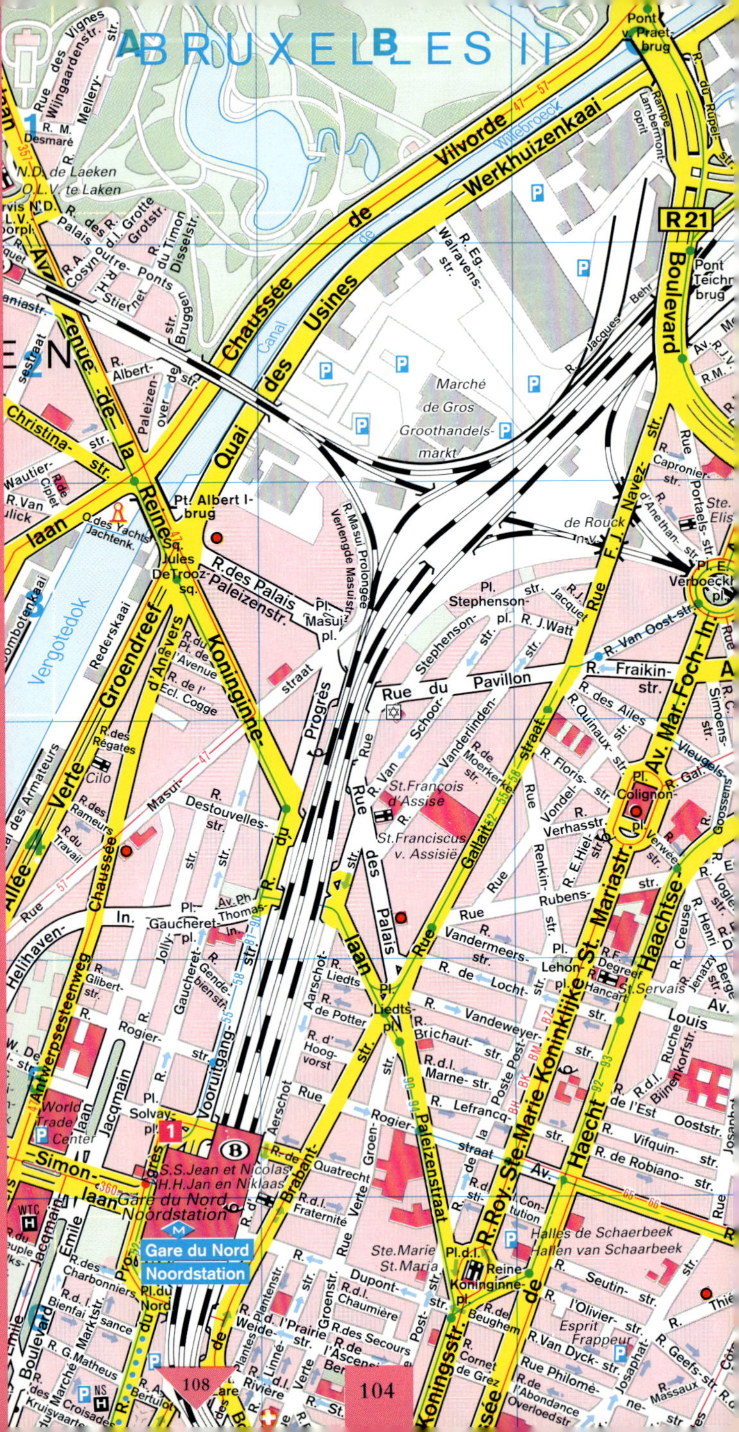
BRUXELLES II
A
B
C
1
2
3
4
5
6
Chaussée de Vilvorde
Werkhuizenkaai
Quai des Usines
Canal
Willebroeck
R 21
Boulevard
Pont v. Praet-brug
Pont Teichm brug
Rampe Lambermont-oprit
R. du Rupel-str.
R. Eg. Walravens-str.
Marché de Gros
Groothandels-markt
R. Jacques
Behr
N.D. de Laeken
O.L.V. te Laken
R. des Palais outre-Ponts
R. M. Desmaré
Rue des Wijngaardenstr.
Mellery-str.
R. A. Cosyn
R. H. Stiernet
R. du Timon Disselstr.
R. Brugges-str.
R. Albert-str.
Paleizen-over
Avenue de la Reine
Koninginnelaan
Christina-str.
Wautier-str.
R. Van Gulick
R. de Ciplet
Pt. Albert I-brug
Q. des Yachts Jachtenk.
Sq. Jules De Trooz-sq.
R. des Palais
Paleizenstr.
Pl. Masui-pl.
R. Masui Prolongée
Verlengde Masuistr.
Vergotedok
Rederskaai
Groendreef
Allée Verte
Koninginne-
R. du Pt. de l'Avenue
R. de l'Ecl. Cogge
Rue du Progrès
straat
Pl. Stephenson-pl.
Stephenson-str.
R. J. Watt
R. J. Jacquet
Rue du Pavillon
R. Van Schoor-str.
Vanderlinden-str.
R. de Moerkerke-str.
St. François d'Assise
St. Franciscus v. Assisië
Rue des Palais
Rue Gallait-straat
Rue F. J. Navez-str.
R. d'Anethan-str.
R. Capronier-str.
Rue Portaels-str.
Ste. Elis
de Rouck
Pl. E. Verboeckh. pl.
R. Van Oost-str.
R. Fraikin-str.
R. des Ailes
R. Quinaux-str.
R. Floris-str.
Vondel-str.
R. Verhasstr.
Pl. Colignon-pl.
Av. Mar. Foch-ln.
Simoens-str.
Vleugels-str.
R. Gal.
Goossens
Verwée-str.
R. Destouvelles-str.
Masui-
R. des Régates
Cilo
R. des Rameurs
R. du Travail
R. des Armateurs
Chaussée d'Anvers
Antwerpsesteenweg
Helihaven-ln.
Pl. Gaucheret-pl.
Av. Ph. Thomas-ln.
Jolly-str.
Gaucheret-str.
R. Gende-bienstr.
R. Glibert-str.
R. Rogier-str.
Vooruitgang-str.
Pl. Solvay-pl.
World Trade Center
Simon-laan
W. De
S.S. Jean et Nicolas
H.H. Jan en Niklaas
Gare du Nord
Noordstation
R. Aarschot
R. Liedts
R. de Potter
R. d'Hoogvorst
Pl. Liedts-pl.
Rue Rogier-straat
R. Vandermeers-str.
R. de Locht-str.
R. Vandeweyer-str.
R. Brichaut-str.
R. d.l. Marne-str.
R. Lefrancq-str.
Poste Post-
Rue Renkin-str.
R. E. Hiel-str.
Rubens-str.
Pl. Lehon-pl.
R. F. Degreef
R. Hancart
St. Servais
Rue Ste. Marie Koninklijke St. Mariastr.
Rue Haecht Haachtse-
R. Creuse
R. Henri Jenatzy
Av. Louis Bertrand
R. d.l. Ruche Bijenkorfstr.
R. de l'Est Ooststr.
R. Vifquin-str.
R. de Robiano-str.
Rue Paleizenstraat
Quatrecht
R. d.l. Fraternité
Rue Verte Groen-
Ste. Marie St. Maria
R. Dupont-str.
R. d.l. Chaumière
R. Royale
Koningsstr.
Pl. d.l. Reine Koninginne-pl.
Halles de Schaerbeek
Hallen van Schaarbeek
R. de la Constitution
R. Seutin-str.
R. l'Olivier-str.
R. Esprit Frappeur
R. Van Dyck-str.
R. Josaphat-
R. Geefs-str.
R. Massaux
Rue Philomène-str.
R. de l'Abondance Overloedstr.
R. Cornet de Grez
R. del Beughem
R.d.l. Prairie
R. des Secours
R. de l'Ascension
R. Plantes
R. Linné
R. d.l. Rivière
R. des Charbonniers
Pl. du Nord
R. d.l. Bienfaisance
R. G. Matheus
R. Marché des Croisades Kruisvaarders
Boulevard Emile Jacqmain
Rue Brabant-
Pl. du Progrès
Thié
108
104

D
E
F
1
2
3
4
5
6
250 m
Parc
Bon Paste
Goede He
Zenne
Rue de Vilvorde
Rampe du Lion
Pont Albert-brug
R. du Château
R. Walckiers-str.
R. Carli-str.
Stroobantsstraat
Schaerbeek
Schaerbeek
23
93
Av. G. Rodenbach-ln.
Av. Z. Gramme-ln.
R. A. Snieders-str.
R. Anatole France-str.
Jaurès-ln.
R. Chaumontel-str.
Rue du Tilleul
Rue J.F.De Craen str.
Gastendellevoetweg
Rue Picardie-str.
R. du Doolegt-str.
Pl. Prs.Elisabeth-pl.
68
Av. Col. Picquart-ln.
Av. Jean Jaurès-ln.
Av.M.Maeterlinck-ln.
R. V. Droogenbroeck
R.S. Pierron
Ch. Séverin-str.
Meert-str.
R. P. Alderson
F. Verdonck
R. H. Van Hamme-str.
Rue Edouard Stuckens
HELMET
Av. Huart Hamoir-ln.
Av. Emile Zola-ln.
R.I. Gilkin-str.
Giraud-ln.
Eekhoud-
R.G. Leroy
R.G. F. Hubert
Rue Bryère Heide-str.
Chaussée de Helmet
R. M. de Wiele
R. G. Gezelle-str.
Rue W. Van Perck
R. P. Mattheusens-str.
R. V. Obberghen-str.
R. H. Van Ne
R.Jacque
Ballin
Av. Albert
E. Verhaeren-ln.
Av. Sleeckx-ln.
Sq. François Riga-sq.
Ste. Famille
H.Familie
R. Ch. Van Lerberghe-str.
Rue du Corbeau
Rue de Lambotte-str.
Raafstr.
R.du Moulin à Vent
Wind-molen-str.
Av. Demolder-ln.
R. du Dahlia-str.
Teleph.
R. J.Blockx-str.
N. de Tière-str.
Helmetsesteenweg
Pl.de Helmet-sepl.
R. Vandevelde-
R. G. Raeymaekers
Henri Jacobs-str.
R.St. Streuvels
Chaussée de Haecht
Sq.de l'Accueil
Onthaalt-sq.
Herto gswegel
Rue Dr. Elie Lambotte
R. A.Detienne-str.
l'Agriculture
R.du Foyer Schaerbeekois
Schaarbeekse Haardstr.
Av. A. Desenfans-ln.
R.L. Courouble-str.
Waelhem-str.
Centre hospitalier
Paul Brien
Hospitaalcentrum
Ch. de Helmet
Av. Lambermont-ln.
Landbouwstr.
Marbotin-str.
Jules Destrée-str.
Linde-
R.d.l. Ré-Weer-str.
R.J.Houtman
R.J.B. Mosselmans-str.
R.G.Kurthstr.
R. Jacques Rayé
Av.U. Britsiers-ln.
Ad.
Av. Dr. Dejase-ln.
R. W. Kuhnen-str.
R. Joseph Wauters-str.
R.A. De Boeck-straat
SCHAARBEEK
Steenweg
Av. Voltaire-ln.
Av. Ernest Renan-ln.
Suffrage Universel
Algemeen Stemrecht-ln.
Av. du
R. T. Coopman
R. Ch. Cramer
Vanderstappen
Pl. Terdelt-pl.
R. J. B. Brems-str.
Av. G.Kennis-str.
66
Cap. Claesstr.
R. P. Theunis
R. A. deRoo
G. Guffens-str.
R. J. Hoste-str.
A.De
Av. R. Foucart-ln.
R.H.Richir str.
R.V. Vanderhoeft
Krains-str.
Desmet-
Pl.de Houffalize-pl.
Av. des Glycines
Blauweregen-ln.
Ste. Suzanne
Drève du Recteur Van Waeyenbergh dr.
Parc Albert I-park
R. D.
Av. Gilisquet-ln.
Bertrand
Av.des Capucines
Kapucijnbloemenln.
All. des Freesias
Av. Gustave Latinis
Cl.du Chemin Creux
Chem. du Forgeron
R. A. Roland-str.
R. Louis
Av. Amb. Van Vollenhoven-ln.
Av. des Héliotropes
Heliotropenln.
Mimosas-
Jacinthes
Hyacinthenln.
Av.des Pensées
Gare Josaphat
Station
E.Fiers-str.
Av. Deschanel-ln.
N21
Parc Josaphat-park
Clinique Lambermont-Kliniek
Av. des Azalées
Azaleaelaan
des Paquerettes
Madeliefjesstr.
R. J. Fontaine d'Amour
Impens-
Bd. Général Wahis
Av. Ch. Ernest Cambier
Stade Communal
Sq. Prévost-Delaunay-sq.
Av. Gal. D. Eisenhower-ln.
R. G. Devresse
R. F. Binjéstr.
Av. J. Stobbaerts-ln.
R. Vandenbussche-str.
R.P. Devigne
Sq. E. Duployé-sq.
Pl. des Bienfaiteurs
R. E.Smits-str.
Dailly
Av. Chazal
Av. des Jardins
Av. des Jeunesse
SCHAERBEEK
105
109
Pl. d.l. Patrie
Vaderlands-
Pavots
Papa-
Monrose-
V. Hamme
Gråde.
Kelbach

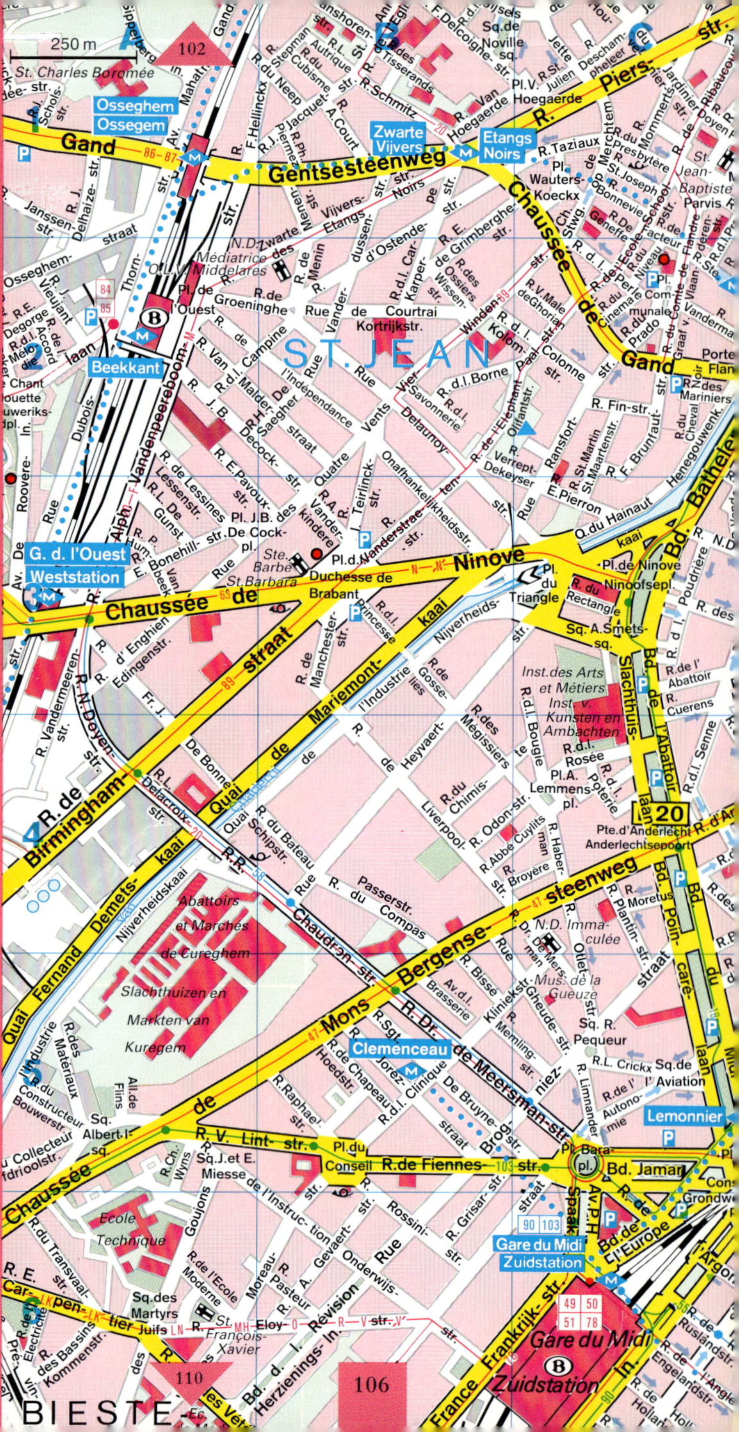

102
250 m
St. Charles Boromée
Osseghem
Ossegem
Gand
Gentsesteenweg
Zwarte Vijvers
Etangs Noirs
R. Piers-str.
Hoegaerde
R. Taziaux
Pl. Wauters-Koeckx
Chaussée de Gand
St. Jean-Baptiste
Parvis
N.D. Médiatrice
O.L.V. Middelares
Pl. de l'Ouest
R. de Groeninghe
Rue de Courtrai
Kortrijkstr.
ST. JEAN
Beekkant
84
85
Vandenpeereboom
R. d. l'Indépendance
R. des Quatre Vents
Onafhankelijkheidsstr.
R. Ransfort
R. Fin-str.
Porte de Flandre
R. des Mariniers
O. du Hainaut
Henegouwenkaai
Bd. Barthélémy
G. d. l'Ouest
Weststation
Ste. Barbe
St. Barbara
Pl. d. Duchesse de Brabant
Chaussée de Ninove
Pl. de Ninove
Ninoofsepl.
Pl. du Triangle
R. du Rectangle
Sq. A. Smets-sq.
Quai de Mariemont-kaai
Inst. des Arts et Métiers
Inst. v. Kunsten en Ambachten
Bd. de l'Abattoir
Slachthuislaan
20
Pte. d'Anderlecht
Anderlechtsepoort
R. de Birmingham
Quai Fernand Demets-kaai
Nijverheidskaai
Abattoirs et Marchés de Cureghem
Slachthuizen en Markten van Kuregem
Chaussée de Mons
Bergensesteenweg
R. Dr. de Meersman-str.
Clemenceau
N.D. Immaculée
Mus. de la Gueuze
Sq. R. Pequeur
Bd. Poincaré-laan
Lemonnier
Sq. de l'Aviation
R.V. Lint-str.
Pl. du Conseil
R. de Fiennes-str.
Pl. Bara
Bd. Jamar
Sq. Albert I-sq.
Sq. J. et E. Miesse
Ecole Technique
R. de l'Instruction
Rue Rossini
90 103
Gare du Midi
Zuidstation
Bd. de l'Europe
Sq. des Martyrs Juifs
St. François-Xavier
R. Eloy
49 50
51 78
Gare du Midi
Zuidstation
France Frankrijk-str.
110
106
BIESTE

103
107
111
Gare du Nord
Noordstation
Yser
Ijzer
Rogier
Flandre
Vlaand.
St.-Katelijne
Ste-Catherine
De Brouckère
Bourse
Beurs
Gare Centr.
Centr. Station
Anneesens
Porte de Namur
Naamse Poort
Louise
Louiza
BRUSSEL
LE SABLON
LES MAROLLES
Bd. du 9e de Ligne
Bd. E. Jacqmain-ln.
Bd. Anspach-ln.
Bd. de l'Empereur
Bd. de l'Impératrice
Bd. Pacheco-ln.
Bd. Berlaimont
R. de la Régence
R. de Namur
R. Haute
R. Blaes
R. Neuve
Pl. De Brouckère
Grd.Pl.
Grote Markt
Hôtel de Ville
Pl.d.l. Monnaie
La Monnaie
Théâtre Flamand
Inst. Pacheco
Grd.Hospice
Pl.des Martyrs
Mont des Arts
Pl. Royale
Palais de Justice
Justitie-paleis
Pl. Poelaert
Parc de Bruxelles
Park v.
Jardin Botanique
Pl. Rogier
Manneken Pis
St.Michel
Ste.-Gudule
Pl.d.l. Chapelle
Grd.Sablon
Pl.du Petit Sablon
Palais d'Egmont
Jardins d'Egmont
Egmont-tuinen
Hôpital St.Pierre
Pl. Rouppe
Pl.de Dinant
Pl. Fontainas
Pl. des Ursulines
Pl.du Jeu de Balle
Pl. Louise
Pl.d.l. Justice
Bibl. Albert I.
Mus. d'Art Moderne
Mus.d'Art Ancien
St.Jacques sur-Coudenberg
Congrès
Colonne du Congrès
Banque Nationale
Clinique St.Jean
N.D.du Finistère
N.D.du Sablon
N.D.d.l. Chapelle
Tour Noire
St.Nicolas
Maison du Roi
St.Géry
N.D.aux Riches-Claires
Ste. Catherine
St.Jean-Baptiste
Pl.du Béguinage
Quai aux Briques
Pl. Ste. Catherine
Vieux Marché aux Grains
Nouv. Marché aux Grains
Pl.Jardins aux Fleurs
R. Dansaert
R. de Flandre
R. Lebeau
R. Royale
Pl. des Palais
R. Ravenstein
Cour des Comptes
R. Brederode
Pl. de l'Albertine
Carr. de l'Europe
Pl.St. Jean
Galerie Ravenstein
Palais Royal

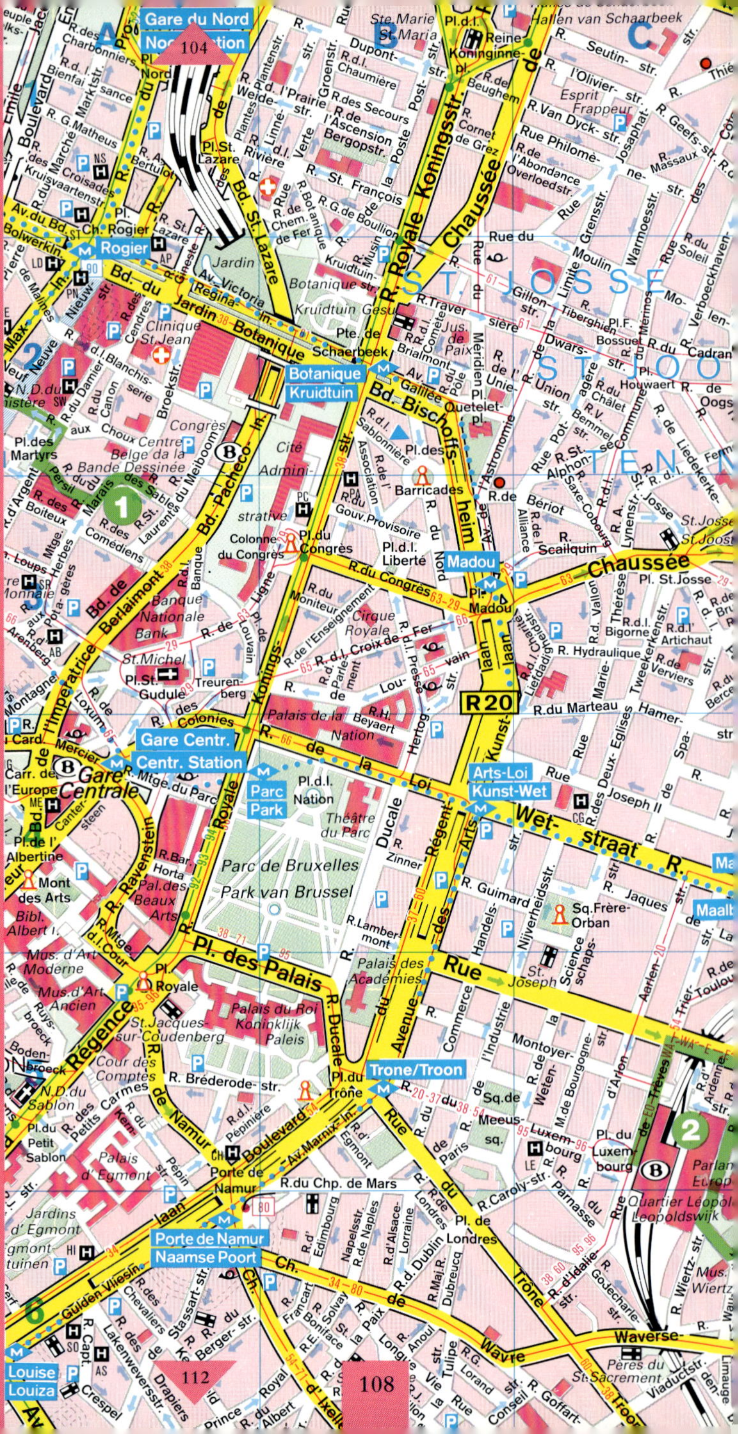

Gare du Nord
Noordstation
104
Ste.Marie
St.Maria
Hallen van Schaarbeek
Rogier
Botanique
Kruidtuin
Madou
Gare Centr.
Centr. Station
Parc
Park
Arts-Loi
Kunst-Wet
Trone/Troon
Porte de Namur
Naamse Poort
Louise
Louiza
ST. JOSSE
ST. JOOST
TEN
R20
Parc de Bruxelles
Park van Brussel
Palais de la Nation
Palais du Roi
Koninklijk Paleis
Palais des Académies
Cité Administrative
Colonne du Congrès
Pl.du Congrès
Banque Nationale Bank
St.Michel
Pl.St. Gudule
Théâtre du Parc
Cirque Royale
Barricades
Pl. des Palais
Pl. Royale
Mus. d'Art Moderne
Mus.d'Art Ancien
St.Jacques-sur-Coudenberg
Bibl. Albert I.
Mont des Arts
Palais d' Egmont
Jardins d' Egmont
Jardin Botanique
Bd. du Jardin Botanique
Bd. St. Lazare
Bd. Pacheco
Bd. Bischoffsheim
Bd. de l'Impératrice
Bd. de Berlaimont
R. Royale
Koningsstr.
Chaussée
Rue de la Loi
Wetstraat
Rue Joseph
Rue Ducale
Avenue des Arts
Régence
Sq.Frère-Orban
Quartier Léopold
Leopoldswijk
Pl. du Luxembourg
Sq.de Meeus
Pl. de Londres
Pl. St.Josse
Pères du St.Sacrement
112
108

105

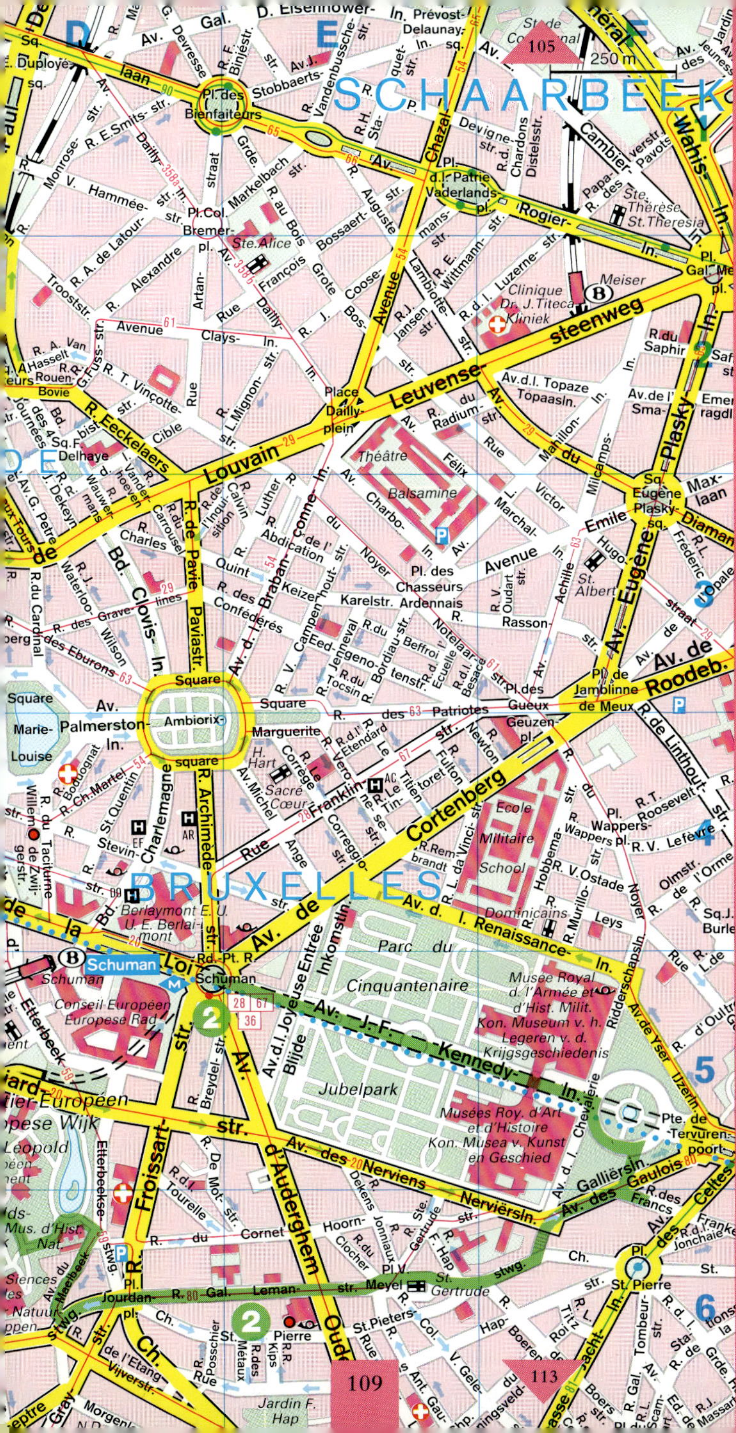

SCHAARBEEK
BRUXELLES
250 m
Pl. des Bienfaiteurs
Pl. d. l. Patrie Vaderlands-pl.
Pl. Col. Bremer-pl.
Ste. Alice
Av. Rogier-ln.
Ste. Thérèse St. Theresia
Meiser
Clinique Dr. J. Titeca Kliniek
Leuvense-steenweg
Place Dailly-plein
Théâtre Balsamine
Sq. Eugène Plasky-sq.
Louvain
Pl. des Chasseurs Ardennais
Av. Eugène Plasky
St. Albert
Square Ambiorix
Square Marie-Louise
Av. Palmerston-ln.
Square Marguerite
Pl. de Jamblinne de Meux
Pl. des Gueux Geuzen-pl.
Av. de Roodeb.
R. de Linthout-str.
Av. de Cortenberg
Ecole Militaire School
Pl. Wappers-pl.
Sacré Cœur
Berlaymont E.U. U.E. Berlai-mont
Schuman
Rd.-Pt. R. Schuman
Conseil Européen Europese Raad
Parc du Cinquantenaire
Jubelpark
Musée Royal d. l'Armée et d'Hist. Milit. Kon. Museum v. h. Legeren v. d. Krijgsgeschiedenis
Musées Roy. d'Art et d'Histoire Kon. Musea v. Kunst en Geschied
Av. J.-F. Kennedy-ln.
Av. d. l. Renaissance-ln.
Pte. de Tervuren-poort
Av. des Nerviens Nerviërsln.
Av. des Gaulois Galliërsln.
Av. d'Auderghem
R. Froissart
Mus. d'Hist. Nat.
Pl. Jourdan-pl.
Pl. V. Meyel
St. Gertrude
Pl. St. Pierre
St. Pierre
Jardin F. Hap
R. Archimède-str.
R. de Pavie Paviastr.
Bd. Clovis-ln.
Av. Michel Ange
R. de la Loi
Etterbeek
Quartier Européen Europese Wijk

113

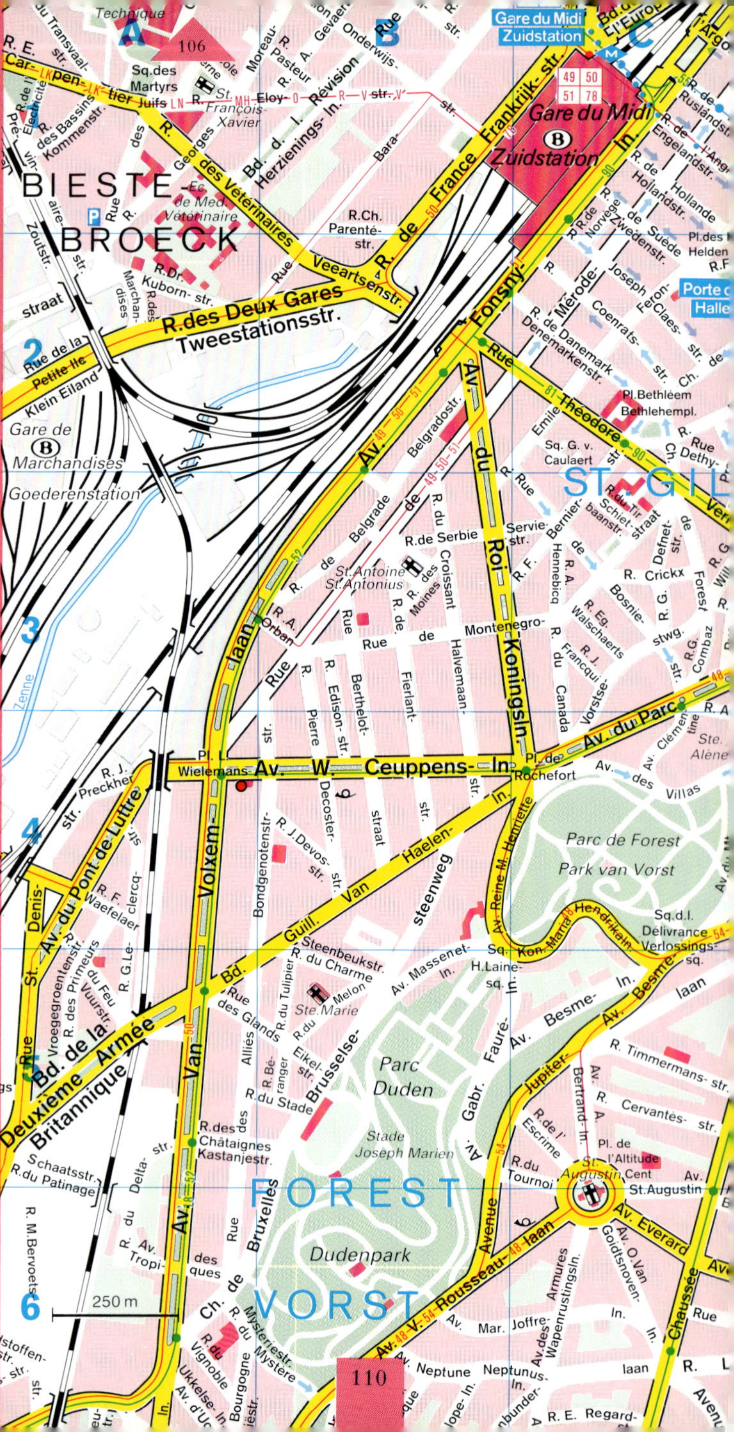
106
110
Gare du Midi
Zuidstation
BIESTE-
BROECK
R.des Deux Gares
Tweestationsstr.
Gare de Marchandises
Goederenstation
R. de France
Frankrijk-str.
R. des Vétérinaires
Veeartsenstr.
Fonsny-
Av.
laan
Av. du Roi
Koningsln.
Rue Théodore
Pl.Bethléem
Bethlehempl.
ST-GILLES
Rue de Belgrade
Rue de Montenegro
R.de Serbie
St.Antoine
St.Antonius
Pl. L. Wielemans
Av. W. Ceuppens-ln.
Pl. de Rochefort
Av. du Parc
Av. des Villas
Parc de Forest
Park van Vorst
Sq.d.l. Délivrance
Verlossings-sq.
Bd. Guill. Van Haelen-
Av. Van Volxem-
Bd. de la Deuxième Armée Britannique
Av. du Pont de Luttre
Ste.Marie
Parc Duden
Stade Joseph Marien
Dudenpark
FOREST
VORST
St.Augustin
Av. Everard
Av. Besme-
Av. Jupiter-
Av. Rousseau-laan
Av. Gabr. Fauré-
Ch. de Bruxelles
Brusselse-steenweg
R.du Patinage
Schaatsstr.
R.des Châtaignes
Kastanjestr.
R.du Stade
Pl. de l'Altitude
Porte de Halle
Sq. G. v. Caulaert
Sq. des Martyrs Juifs
Bd. d. l. Révision
Herzienings-ln.
Rue de la Petite Ile
Klein Eiland
250 m
2
3
4
5
6
A
B
C

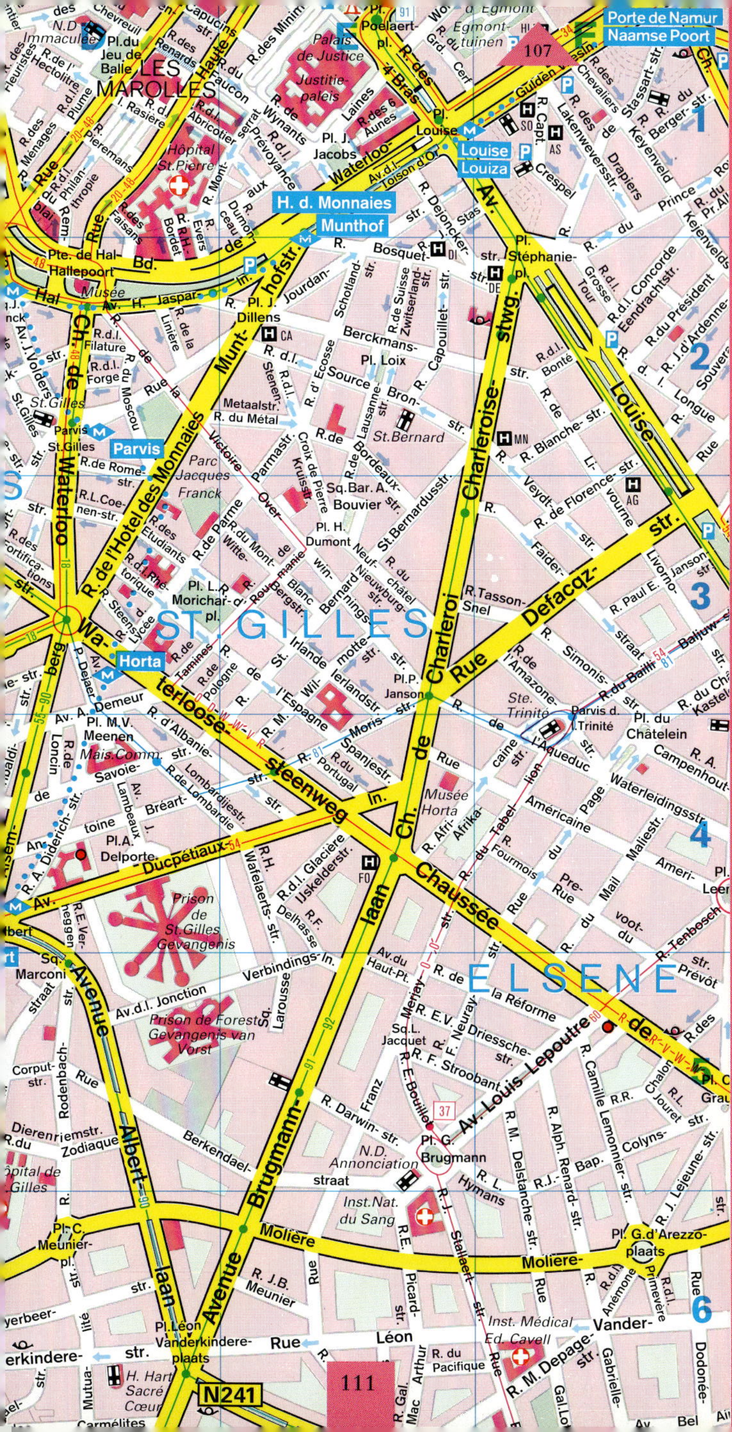

Porte de Namur
Naamse Poort
107
LES MAROLLES
Palais de Justice
Justitie-paleis
Hôpital St.Pierre
Pl. Louise
Louise
Louiza
H. d. Monnaies
Munthof
Pte. de Hal
Halleport
Musée
Bd. de Waterloo
Av. Louise
Pl. Stéphanie
Pl. J. Dillens
Pl. Loix
St.Bernard
Parvis
St.Gilles
Parc Jacques Franck
Sq. Bar. A. Bouvier
Pl. H. Dumont
Pl. L. Morichar-pl.
ST. GILLES
Horta
Ch. de Waterloo
Waterloose-steenweg
Ch. de Charleroi
Charleroise-stwg.
Rue Defacqz-str.
Pl. P. Janson
Ste. Trinité
Parvis d. l.Trinité
Pl. du Châtelein
Pl. M.V. Meenen
Mais.Comm.
Pl. A. Delporte
Av. Ducpétiaux
Prison de St.Gilles Gevangenis
Musée Horta
Chaussée de Waterloo
Sq. Marconi
Prison de Forest Gevangenis van Vorst
Av. d. l. Jonction
Av. Albert-laan
Av. Brugmann-laan
ELSENE
Av. Louis Lepoutre
Pl. G. Brugmann
N.D. Annonciation
Inst.Nat. du Sang
Rue Molière
Pl. G.d'Arezzo-plaats
Inst. Médical Ed. Cavell
Pl. Léon Vanderkindere-plaats
H. Hart Sacré Cœur
N241
111
1
2
3
4
5
6

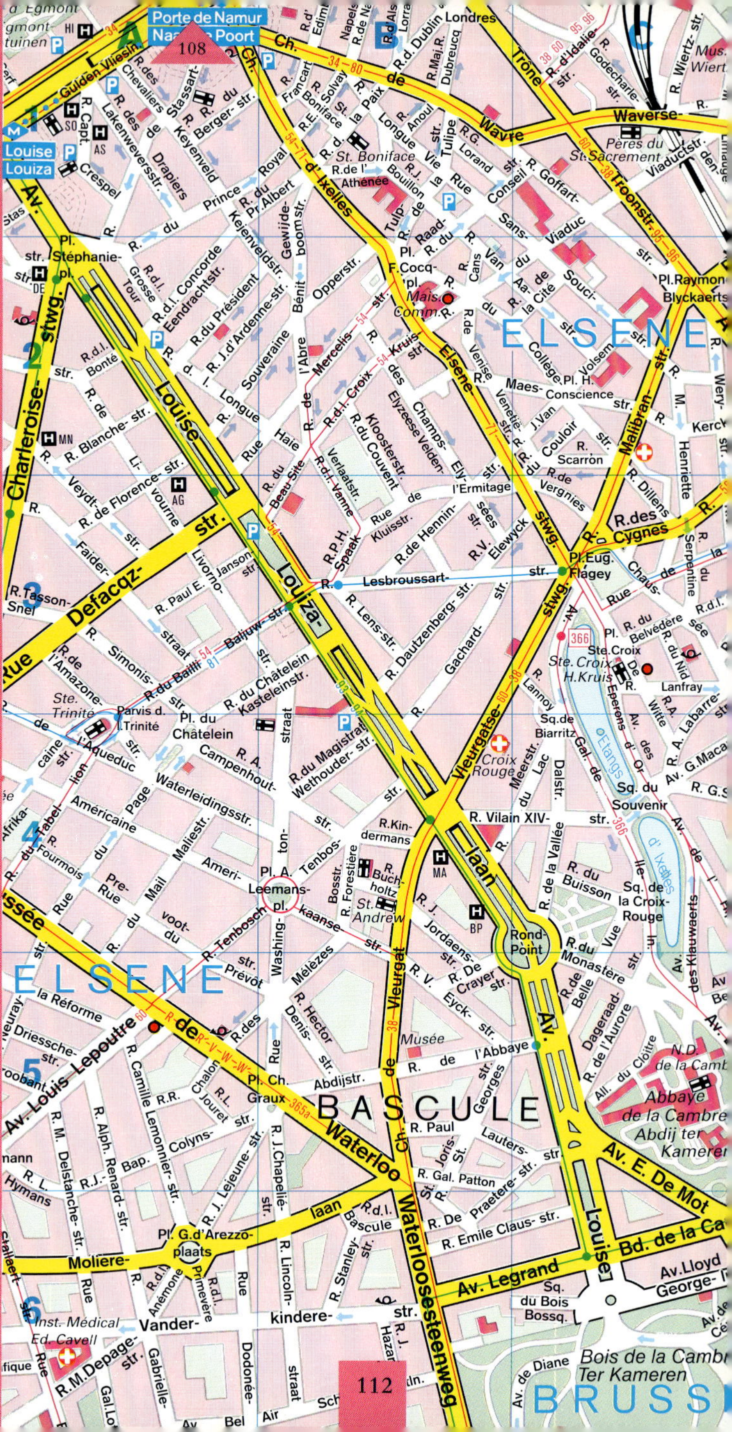

Porte de Namur
Naamse Poort
108
A
B
C
Egmont
Egmont-tuinen
Louise
Louiza
Gulden Vliesin.
R. des Chevaliers
R. des Drapiers
Lakenweversstr.
Stassart-str.
R. du Berger-str.
Keyenveld
R. Capt. Crespel
Ch. de Wavre
Waverse-
Rue Royal
Prince Albert
R. du Pr. Albert
Ch. d'Ixelles
Elsene-stwg.
St. Boniface
R. de l'Athenée
R. Francart
R. Solvay
R. de la Paix
R. Longue Vie
R. de la Tulipe
R. Goffart-str.
R. Sans-Souci
Viaduc
Viaductstr.
Pères du St. Sacrement
Troonstr.
Trône
R. Wiertz-str.
R. Godecharle-str.
R. d'Idalie-str.
R. Dublin
Londres
Mus. Wiertz
Pl. Raymond Blyckaerts
Pl. Stéphanie-pl.
Charleroise-stwg.
R. de la Concorde
Eendrachtstr.
R. du Président
R. J. d'Ardenne-str.
R. Souveraine
R. Longue Haie
Pl. F. Cocq-pl.
Mais. Comm.
R. de la Cité
R. du Collège
R. Van Aa
Opperstr.
R. Mercelis-str.
R. de la Croix
R. du Couvent
Kloosterstr.
R. des Champs-Elysées
Elyzeese Velden-str.
ELSENE
R. Malibran
Pl. H. Conscience
R. Maes-str.
R. de Venise
Venetië-str.
R. Scarron
R. Couloir
R. de Vergnies
R. Dillens
R. des Cygnes
R. Henriette
R. Wery-str.
R. Kerckx
R. Blanche-str.
R. de Florence-str.
R. Veydt-
R. Faider-str.
R. de Livourne
R. du Beau Site
R. de l'Ermitage
R. de Hennin
R. P. H. Spaak
Rue Kluisstr.
R. Lesbroussart-str.
Pl. Eug. Flagey
R. Lens-str.
R. Dautzenberg-str.
R. Gachard-str.
R. Paul E. Janson-str.
Rue Defacqz-str.
R. Tasson-Snel
R. Simonis-straat
R. de l'Amazone-str.
R. du Bailli
Baljuw-str.
R. du Châtelein
Kasteleinstr.
Pl. du Châtelein
Ste. Trinité
Parvis d. l. Trinité
R. de l'Aqueduc
Waterleidingsstr.
R. A. Campenhout-str.
R. du Magistrat
Wethouder-str.
Vleurgatse-stwg.
R. Lannoy
Sq. de Biarritz
Croix Rouge
R. du Lac
Meerstr.
Dalstr.
Gal. de
Étangs d'Ixelles
Sq. du Souvenir
Ste. Croix
H. Kruis
Pl. Ste. Croix
R. du Belvédère
R. du Nid
R. Lanfray
R. A. Labarre-str.
Av. G. Macau
Av. des Éperons d'Or
R. Vilain XIV-str.
R. Kindermans
R. de la Vallée
R. du Buisson
Sq. de la Croix-Rouge
Av. des Klauwaerts
R. Américaine
R. du Tabellion
R. Fourmois
R. du Page
Maliestr.
Pl. A. Leemans-pl.
R. Tenbosch
Tenbos-
Washington-str.
R. Forestière
Bosstr.
R. Buchholtz
St. Andrew
R. J. Jordaens-str.
Rond-Point
R. du Monastère
R. de la Belle
Vue
Dageraad-
R. de l'Aurore
R. V. Eyck-str.
R. De Crayer
R. Mélèzes
R. Hector Denis-str.
Musée
R. de l'Abbaye
Abdijstr.
ELSENE
R. de la Réforme
R. Driessche-str.
Av. Louis Lepoutre
R. Camille Lemonnier-str.
R. Prévot
Pl. Ch. Graux
Chaussée de Waterloo
Waterloosesteenweg
BASCULE
R. Paul Lauters-str.
R. Joris-St.
R. Gal. Patton
R. Praetere-str.
R. Emile Claus-str.
R. de Bascule
R. Stanley-str.
Av. Legrand
Bd. de la Cambre
Av. E. De Mot
Av. Lloyd George
Av. Louise
Louizalaan
N.D. de la Cambre
Abbaye de la Cambre
Abdij ter Kameren
All. du Cloître
R. Alph. Renard-str.
R. M. Delstanche-str.
R. J. Lejeune-str.
R. J. Chapelié-str.
R. Lincoln-str.
Pl. G. d'Arezzo-plaats
Molière-
Vanderkindere-str.
Inst. Médical Ed. Cavell
R. M. Depage-str.
Gabrielle-
Dodonée-
Sq. du Bois
Bossq.
Bois de la Cambre
Ter Kameren
Av. de Diane
BRUSS
MA
BP
MN
AG
AS
SO
DE
1
2
3
4
5
6

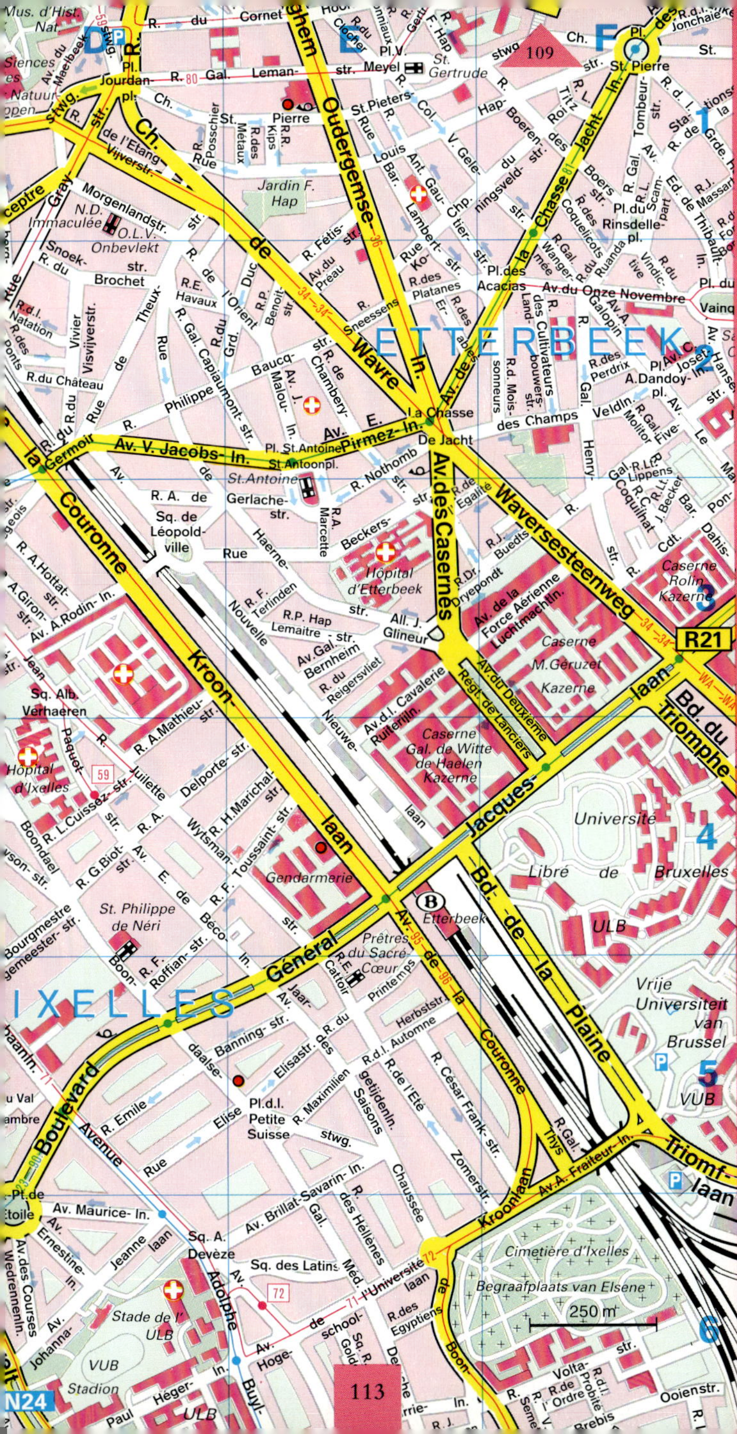

109
113
D
E
F
1
2
3
4
5
6
ETTERBEEK
IXELLES
Chaussée de Wavre
Oudergemse-stwg.
Av. de la Chasse
Jachtln.
Waversesteenweg
Av. des Casernes
Bd. du Triomphe
Triomflaan
Bd. de la Plaine
Kroonlaan
Av. de la Couronne
Boulevard Général Jacques
Generaal Jacqueslaan
Av. V. Jacobs-ln.
Av. E. Pirmez-ln.
Pl. St.Antoine
St.Antoonpl.
St.Antoine
La Chasse
De Jacht
Jardin F. Hap
Pl.V. Meyel
St. Gertrude
St. Pierre
N.D. Immaculée
O.L.V. Onbevlekt
Morgenlandstr.
Sq. de Léopoldville
Hôpital d'Etterbeek
Hôpital d'Ixelles
Sq. Alb. Verhaeren
Caserne Rolin Kazerne
Caserne M.Geruzet Kazerne
Caserne Gal. de Witte de Haelen Kazerne
Av. de la Force Aérienne
Luchtmachtln.
Av. du Deuxième Régt. de Lanciers
Gendarmerie
Etterbeek
Université Libre de Bruxelles
ULB
Vrije Universiteit van Brussel
VUB
Prêtres du Sacré-Cœur
St. Philippe de Néri
Pl.d.l. Petite Suisse
Cimetière d'Ixelles
Begraafplaats van Elsene
250 m
R21
N24
Stade de l'ULB
VUB Stadion
Av. Maurice-ln.
Av. Brillat-Savarin-ln.
Av. A.Fraiteur-ln.
Av. de l'Université
Universiteitslaan
Av. des Acacias
Av. du Onze Novembre
Av. A. Rodin-ln.

STREET ATLAS LEGEND

Autoroute avec numéro d'échangeur Autobahn mit Nr. der Autobahnanschlußstelle	Motorway with number of junction Autosnelweg met Nummer van op-en afritten
Route à quatre voies Vierspurige Straße	Road with four lanes Weg met vier rijstroken
Route nationale ou à grande circulation Fernstraße	Federal road or trunk road Rijksweg of weg voor interlokaal verkeer
Route principale Hauptstraße	Main road Hoofdweg
Autres routes Sonstige Straßen	Other roads Overige wegen
Parking - Information Parkplatz - Information	Parking place - Information Parkeerplaats - Informatie
Rue à sens unique - Zone piétonne Einbahnstraße - Fußgängerzone	One way road - Pedestrian zone Straat met éénrichtingsverkeer - Voetgangerzone
Chemin de fer principal avec gare Hauptbahn mit Bahnhof	Main railway with station Belangrijke spoorweg met station
Autres lignes Sonstige Bahnen	Other railways Ondergrondse spoorweg
Métro U-Bahn	Subway Overige spoorwegen
Tramway - Ligne d'autobus Straßenbahn - Buslinie	Tramway - Bus-route Tram - Omnibuslijn
Église remarquable - Autres églises Sehenswerte Kirche - Sonstige Kirchen	Church of interest - Other churches Bezienswaardige kerk - Andere kerken
Synagogue Synagoge	Synagogue Synagoge
Monument - Auberge de jeunesse Denkmal - Jugendherberge	Monument - Youth hostel Monument - Jeugdherberg
Poste de police - Bureau de poste Polizeistation - Postamt	Police station - Post office Politiebureau - Postkantoor
Hôpital - Hôtel Krankenhaus - Hotel	Hospital - Hotel Ziekenhuis - Hotel
Zones bâties, edifice public Bebauung, öffentliches Gebäude	Built-up area, public building Woongebied, openbaare gebouwen
Zone industrielle Industriegebiet	Industrial area Industriekomplex
Parc, bois Park, Wald	Park, forest Park, bos

200 m

Marco Polo Walking Tours

1. Wall paintings: on the trail of world-famous comic heroes
2. Jubilee Park and a visit to Europe in the "Cheese Box"

STREET ATLAS INDEX

This index lists a selection of the streets and squares shown in the Street Atlas.

INDEX

This index lists all the main sights and restaurants mentioned in this guide. Numbers in bold indicate a main entry, italics a photograph.

What do you get for your money?

Bank notes are in denominations of Bfr 100, 200, 500, 1,000, 2,000 and 5,000 and coins to the value of Bfr 1, 5, 20 and 50.

Eurocheques can be made out up to a total of Bfr 7,000. Almost all hotels, restaurants, high-quality shops and car rental firms accept credit cards.

Opera and theatre tickets cost between Bfr 300 and 6,200, and cinema tickets between Bfr 190 and 250. It costs Bfr 50 to travel on the Metro, and an espresso on the terrace costs Bfr 65, whilst a small beer costs Bfr 55 or, on the terrace, Bfr 75. Postage is Bfr 17 for a postcard, and 250 g of chocolates cost from Bfr 125 upwards. The minimum taxi fare is Bfr 95. A freshly baked "Brussels waffle" from a waffle stand costs Bfr 55. In restaurants the *plat du jour* (dish of the day) costs approximately Bfr 355, whilst you should expect to pay about Bfr 850 for a full meal consisting of several courses. Admission to museums ranges from being free to costing Bfr 300.

US$	Bfr	£	Bfr	Can $	Bfr
1	43.07	1	67.99	1	29.16
2	86.14	2	135.98	2	58.32
3	129.21	3	203.97	3	87.48
4	172.28	4	271.96	4	116.64
5	215.35	5	339.95	5	145.80
10	430.70	10	679.90	10	291.60
15	646.05	15	1,019.85	15	437,40
20	861.40	20	1,359.80	20	583.20
25	1,076.75	25	1,699.75	25	729.00
30	1,292.10	30	2,039.70	30	874.80
40	1,722.80	40	2,719.60	40	1,166.40
50	2,153.50	50	3,399.50	50	1,458.00
60	2,584.20	60	4,079.40	60	1,749.60
70	3,014.90	70	4,759.30	70	2,041.20
80	3,445.60	80	5,439.20	80	2,332.80
90	3,876.30	90	6,119.10	90	2,624.40
100	4,307.00	100	6,799.00	100	2,916.00
200	8,614.00	200	13,598.00	200	5,832.00
300	12,921.00	300	20,397.00	300	8,748.00
400	17,228.00	400	27,196.00	400	11,664.00
500	21,535.00	500	33,995.00	500	14,580.00
750	32,302.50	750	50,992.50	750	21,870.00
1,000	43,070.00	1,000	67,990.00	1,000	29,160.00

These exchange rates are for guidance only and are correct at May 2000. You are advised to check with a bank or tourist office before travelling.